# A TRUE ACC

## David Grundy

Published 2023 by the87press

The 87 Press LTD

87 Stonecot Hill

Sutton

Surrey

SM3 9HJ

www.the87press.co.uk

ISBN: 978-1-7393939-5-3

Printed and bound by CPI Group (UK) Ltd, Croydon, CR0 4YY
Cover art © Candace Hill-Montgomery, *Asafoetida*. Japan color on
Arches watercolour paper, 2022.
Design: Stanislava Stoilova [www.sdesign.graphics]

# Praise for *A True Account*

"David Grundy's first full length book offers *A True Account* of a poet who embraces the weighty feeling and guiding power of the Political and the Poetic and their instructive intertwining. Grundy discerns that 'under winter, is another, endless winter', and he writes in and through that season, casting nets at spring. The poems sing out to behold 'the world that could be within the world that is' and to breathe the crisp clean air of could be. To that end, Grundy writes, and I wholeheartedly concur, 'Fuck what pre-/ vents un/ Encumbered breath'."

—Alli Warren, author of *I Love it Though*

"Lyrically gorgeous and real poetry. This book is a bright spot in a bleak time."

—Peter Gizzi, author of *Sky Burial: New and Selected Poems*

"This poetry is the result of an intense and rigorous labour, and the measure of labor is written into this work in a way that cannot be bought or purchased or built out on demand. The movement of that work, the measure and pacing of it, the emotive or affective written into the meter—or what I imagine Zukofsky would call sincerity—is the result of a daily and enduring practice predicated on discipline across a clear measure of time, and so the work has a quality to it that discloses the lived history of both the experience the poem gestures toward and also the poetic discipline that makes the poem possible. The writing bears out through itself its own self in eminently recognizable ways, as the lived and shared material grain of an actual and identifiably distinct human utterance: a sustained manner of poetic being in time, a manner of being that changes with time, in subtle and nuanced ways, as might the bark and viscera of a tree as it lives across time—multiple valences of imagining radiating from the same source as might light or sound."

—Richard Owens, author of *Sauvage: Essays on Anglophone Poetry*

"To critique David Grundy's poetry is difficult to the extent that it does that job itself: it is a thoroughly self-critical, self-conscious, awkward poetry. Grundy's poetry is frequently—and necessarily —overly convoluted, syntactically confusing, wide-ranging, never-ending. Sometimes it stumbles, sometimes it streams (more, more, more – thought live), sometimes it flies—only to hit its head on the Sky® that is a British brick wall, just when you thought you were so close to becoming universal and infinite.

Grundy's recent poems are attempts to understand critically the conditions of the production of our lives in Western European liberal democracy during the first decades of the twenty-first century. Grundy's poetry insists that thought must be articulated from the position of a subject, given that people are determined by non-virtual and non-fluid realities—they live somewhere rather than nowhere, they are obliged to pay their bills, they are bound to families and workplaces. But it also insists that all subjectivity is entirely—without rest—political. To make this point, Grundy's poetry is necessarily damning wherever experience is left to stand naïvely rather than critically understood—and that damning gesture might sometimes feel unbearably hateful and destructive of the possibility of life as such. But to hate ease, sentimentality, false immediacy, contentment with one's self-identity is ultimately a form of love—love expressed in Grundy's precise attention to the inconsistencies in our thought and action, to our unfreedom, to the fact that we are, inescapably, lies in the shape of human bodies. Love as the wish to understand better 'the problem' and 'the condition'. And that love requires 'the problem, the questions, the poem' to be shit insofar as our lives (one big life!) are shit."

—Lisa Jeschke, author of *The Anthology of Poems by Drunk Women*

## ACKNOWLEDGMENTS

Most of these poems were written between 2013 and 2020, and most, though not all, have previously appeared in whole or in part in the magazines *Botch, Brexit / Borders Kill, Datableed, Halfcircle, Gaff, Guestworks, Hi Zero, Mote, No Prizes, SUNDIAL, Sure Hope,* and *Violent Girlfriend,* in the chapbooks *Whatever You Think The Good Home* (Punch Press, 2014), *The Problem, The Questions, The Poem* (Tipped Press, 2015), *To The Reader* (Shit Valley, 2016), and *Relief Efforts* (Barque Press, 2018), and in the anthology *From London Out* (Free Poetry, 2017). My thanks to the editors, and gratitude to all those who have responded to and commented on this work over the years.

# Table of Contents

# ARC POETRY

The treatise begins again:

In politics, there are tactics and modes of organization which must move beyond friendship and whatever we call the 'communities' surrounding our poems in order to have any kind of efficacy—yet poetry itself must rely utterly on precisely those ties. The poet intersects with and passionately draws on the struggles for life that inhere within the forms of socialist politics: but *the poet* is not a political category.

So what is the measure you measure your life by? How do you give count, account of it? The sounding of this line, within and without your head and your mouth, as dialogue, even with the dead. The poem intimately lived through its prosody, its voice; to live up to that truth, for and from and within you. You must change your life so that your poetry changes, and the change in your poetry will itself change your life.

\*

Who *said* this?

Never at any point in my life have I needed poetry MORE, said the person lying in the road on the way from work.

Fucked up, wrecked.

To exaggerate and amplify life to the pitch of liveability. The moment of most intense engagement is also the moment of most intense unhappiness: because seeing the world that could be within the world that is risks amplifying the contradictions to the peak of unbearable promise.

*

What's what in the wasted, blasted earth.

The poem as a beacon flashes on, flashes off, hazards a guess.

The poem of THIS moment, written, read, lived.

Here WE are hearing or reading THIS poem, HERE, *now*, here I am falling OFF the edge of my seat or the edges of our collective seats and ONTO the floor, here is the poet bleeding onto the concrete and still explaining why you must not give up on poetry, finishing their sentence even as they bleed.

THIS is what is real to me now.

*

Everything collapses, everything pulls or falls apart; We may not agree; we *will* not agree; we may violently *dis*agree; but we will test things out, will speak and fail and fall and try it all again.

I tried to say it and it multiplied a thousand ways and splintered and crashed and burned and pick itself up and crawled and ran and exploded.

Arcs and archives. Smoke and mirrors and blinding fire.

*We'll never have any other explanation.*

*2013, revised 2022*

# ENVOY

Let me explain. I missed so many things, and went in all the wrong doors. In the story it ends in a massacre; fuck you, anatomy is not destiny; I never concentrated in biology.

They always say body in the singular.
They always gender in the imperative.

In the poem I love the care with which objects are picked to be generous to in the poem.

We are tender to tear the insides spill out and it's not disgusting, just a little bit.

Infinitive intervention, articulate interview, infinitely pained.

The ships waiting to take us away will sink; with joy to block the port; blow up the ship; in the burning heat of day where heat becomes heart with one letter removed, heart becomes heat, just a little bit.

People talk a lot, but this is private.

Contrast these rooms with nothing, say you want luxury for everyone.

This is not decadent even if I wish.

The names of musicians; of whoever cares to listen. Music that expresses every human wish; obscurity as value; plain written song. Conflict in one voice then resolution in the next; Requests, advice, opinions, oh I don't know, the whole thing. As if to say: actually brilliant; yes, mythologies, multitudes, containers; end the world in a glance and fulfil it;

no one gets back in and no one gets to leave.

# A TRUE ACCOUNT

In the square when it seems
no police would dare to enter there
you might read poems &
drink; this is not strategic
ecstasy but some form of
actual communion uncannibalized,
not riding or sitting but climbing the fence,
& we realized when high that you thought
the correct theorists were "of my father's
generation and not mine", but you have
beaten the English Defence League with a stick and with
your belt and that is absolutely correct what
you did, I am learning from it.
Are also enraged in basic wage labour,
it is your flesh that drapes
the sandwiches, actual particles
of skin flaking in covering.

This is not typology and
the period of purification and trial
as ritual strengthening test,
when there were no other people left
on the earth. My souls, all two hundred
of them, bursting themselves
out of or taking themselves
into me, my free-will exposed &
I have skin for brains &
I have soiled myself within
myself but am cleaner in dirt
than a white banner, or it is
that my banner is
unfurled, painted

in red and waved
as possible love over
the excellent rubbish jamming
the traffic of police forces
before as shit binmen they kicked
the bags away and off runs
my heart in fear to be lost
without tactics, revisiting the
sites of former defeats marked
as glory. In any case, there are
no poems on the underground,
only poets, travelling extensions
collapsing on the pavement like
reprobate decadent friends would
in beautiful idiocy, but whatever,
this poem is a complete and true history
of the end of the universe, a poem of
basic enthusiasm from the eschatological
perspective of the death of god, so that's it.
There's your book.

In the end god decreated himself the heavens
and the earth swallowing him the ocean rising
absolutely red and in the bleeding heart of hope.

You are a revolutionary mystic but that is ok;
I saw no police until there were police vans
confusingly deployed all over the place;
but who confuses who in this following?
I will apply myself to the study of laws
not in existence and dedicate myself to
their initiation, letting off the weak,
un-arresting the arrestees, believing
even in actual justice when I am so drunk.

There was an actual garden climbing up the wall,
an earthly delight you want to alight over every
area of the life of every man woman and child
within this beautiful dream, having lost the bag
with your feelings in it but finding it again
transfigured in the sky which is enormous with a
ghost sun even become the moon; the dog eating
the meat his master has bought will learn to be without
such heinous mastery, an image in which I so
impossibly believe that no more can I speak,
shirtless and shoeless, having dream visions when the
window opens at eight in the morning;
the mill on the floss that fell on the face,
the unrealized heaven of the working class
and of class abolition; it is too early but at least
with clarity of vision we are central to the workings
of the universe and run it forever, oh fuck all rule if in external
internalized lie its law smothers us, breathe the
clear air of completely shitty smell, the boy
stood on the burning plastic bin, extreme
moral obscurity, I can feel the wings.

## SUDDENLY I BENT TO RECEIVE...

Suddenly I bent to receive
full in my face
the rain,
soft and open.

But really this was a hard disguise
not open enough, that we would
still have in our singing,
hammer our mouths parched shut
though still would maybe escape
small shavings of sound from shut lips,
bright or dim, and so terrible
inane saying this
wherever bends the street
to destroyed being, which is
knowing too well full
blind in the absolute sheer
apparence of what is in no way
brilliance,

to be
simply, quiet,

fell away at this curve.

Or it was a too sharp angle,

some others went by,
in at the dark wood
in the middle of
instances
carefully prepared

and hesitating to stumble impaired
by distinct lack of vision,
yet still,
fixating on surfaces or not,
summoning a wider breadth of clarity and under-
standing,
I and the others

didn't fall, or thanks be to
nothing, fell too hard, too
tall the trees would come down with
clumping heaves get stuck at the
point of division: a workman's hand is not
as strong as you hoped would support your
feather weight in reading, and lounging, studying
hard slumped on a sofa all the way down the line with
your finger hungover.

To know this sicked me
in the gut, and loud,
wearing suitable matching
colours for the festival
occasion, to mourn
a passing.

Explain it to them how, in no way final,
the new year promised beauty
and fruit, in its rain, and the spray in the faces raised
round, look!

Willed that of necessity
it be so tough.

Worded wider in call as wild
as to survive.

You can't call.

Because a name escaped.

These are trees that leak.
This is a honey so harsh
it rots the sweetest meat
in glaze.

Hurting in throat rasps
no logical speech, though every hurt
compels and silences in what is not
ever to be figured as measure,
you could not say it a song
though it wanders, could not
adequately see when funnelled to know
too specific not everything,
as it could not be known,
attrition as every means seems already to be broken up.
To cleave to and clasp
at over-stretched seam.

Here the movement shifts
It had better beggar belief.
Joins or secedes, each word
to the next in rhyme
it links so weak,
grasped in hand to fall
down a well that is only
down, or lost, or is it
question or answer

that echo does abide.

And the police are on strike for minor offences
and will continue to kill as no kind save the position they are
embodying.

Save the date, the arbitrary division to time,
symbolic in each occasion we are inside.

Or listen, as a list, as a story told,
objects and people succeeding. As:

- it was a puddle or tears

- a meeting arranged and delayed in the dark

- there was one hard done by with pocket spilled to
  money and a lost watch speaking of hope belied yet
  frozen

- an icicle on the brow, was sweat,
  matched by tears, provoked by wind, smothered coughs
  and excrescences of breath desired in caress
  to take care of things for all good times or protection

- there was one who said at least the best are full of
      passionate pained
  worse fears
  panted in parting

- that these fears worsen and question worth
  as an intense matching to the times
  where the points on the compass line
  up with the map in the head not corresponding to
      perspective
  established by whoever establishes perspective—

- and who does—what will we
    do?

- that day falls fastest as night moves in for the kill
  and we are in deep in that night in temporary want,
    or glut,
  deep down in the gut
  are embodied in its forces as the faces
  behaving for whoever wants to have
  it that way and submitted the body's text—

  formatted with comments

- of the housing question

- written as a good presentable self-
  modelling, enabled to function in the getting of bread
  and the stuffing of notes to the mouth and singing

- there was one rising as to the shade of light and its
    pool and
  the narrows hard to negotiate

- there was one folded the rose collapsed to its
    crushed petals in the lap,
  sprinkled for decoration and scent on the hardened
    damaged floor.


So after all, in the wood, among the leaves or streets,
I went in at the door, saw what's
all the fuss else all else matters none too much,
as acquisition of facts or impressions
spread over widening as a felt territory
where slips to be spat up sharp crunching in again

on itself and soft, and what I was told sucked
and was not enough
to be known or believed,

as when bells go declaratively pealing by
and remaining you hear the sigh
that tells you, still sitting in the hole,
in spite of all
possible modifications in tone,
despite every song sung,
in every possible register and key,
you will turn around and you will see
you have got up and you are alone.

# WHATEVER YOU THINK
# THE GOOD HOME

*if i bring back*
*life to a home of want*
*let it be me. [...]*

*if want & hurt are clothed, bring*
*back life to home. if*
*want decides, let it be me.*

—*A.B. SPELLMAN*

*

To be in the dark,
in the world.
The world, as dark.
To be known in, knowing
this world, unknown.

In the houses the lights go on.
In the dark. Edge.
Who houses. Is housed.
Who comes back
to where they come from.

\*

Who houses
in hurt, in want, the clothed, the full, the walls
press in. In basic need un-pressing, there is the coarser
way, the demand screamed extreme in each
stomach's growl. Be so worthy to be so kind,
so, at rest, home is laid to rest, if in walls the
stretching grave. I mean, it really is, for those that
know the sky, the root fallen in, in heaven up-gazing
on punishment fire agreed to be rained down. So have
your life. Sifting in rubble will be remnants packed,
picked at, as symbol, as token stated line
in grim pretence calls not-life to life.
List. Can it spare a thing.

\*

Is it hard to get up out of sight.
Is it known in mind to be providing graft.
Stutter and lie back. The dawn is dread for those
that know it, shift falls to clothe
want, is hurt, is mere numb. As life
breaks. Night is work where money
goes down. Gets had, but bare,
in pittance remitted, allowed
back in. The gate closes right
if it is earned. In division shuts in.
Will bright night be ever bright,
have or hold any visible thing.

\*

Who hears the fall of a house in a city.
So many times owned. The permanent ones,
on hold, hold safe on. Let
permanence fall, they said, let
permission granted be transition enough,
cupped in the hand. They were the lords of
land, theirs the estate of ages, if anyone hears
whose ears were those, were theirs for sure,
if a house should fall.

# AGAINST NATURE

\*

We need to have the right conversations for poetry.
Everything goes in. EVERYTHING.

I heard the world turns
on a dicey game called instability and the sadness of all
    mutable life,
that all music is beautiful and keeps us alive,
makes the sky fall from its moorings in abjected care;

Wanting poetry to *save* my life, to *shame* my life,
as LONG as the WORLD is WIDE,
and as WIDE as the WORLD is LONG.

\*

The movers and shakers are moving and shaking,
the world in their arms in war is embracing
the extension of conflict in endless invading.

Spring begins within.

All the houses are beautiful, even the shipping containers
        and the sheds.
The gardens are gardens of innocent expulsion. Limitless
        repulsion.

That was NATURE, this is CULTURE:
an expanding world,
relation in contradiction.

Resistance, friendship, love, fire and
Light, in the middle of the night.

Come for the rhyme, stay for the fight.

\*

Because the kind of poetry you write is changing, the world is
changing. Current trends in anti-academic academic poetry.
Current trends in repression in the disguised training-grounds
    of the rich,
My NEW BOOK, coming VERY SOON!
You MUST learn how to live your life properly!
Right now, we are all so perfectly divided.
Pessimism of the intellect, pessimism of the will.

This is my programme for society.
Two roads diverged, passing by woods on a snowy evening:
    the dictatorship of art,
the freedom of art. NONE OF it adds up. Throbbing with
    grief, you have moved to the
moon and they have rented your apartment to someone else.
    Building new forms of art
so that they can convey life. A carefully poised irony,
    dialectically intended.

*One should live as long as is humanly possible.*
The work departs from you, and it preserves you.
Rhyme, the phrase, protect the poet,
the thread, ahead a flickering flame.

\*

I want HEALTH to make me SICK.

Is this reactionary?

WORLD PEACE, come save me with complete catastrophe.
Either the end of all things,
or bliss for all time.

Banging your shoe on the table, banging your *table* on the table,
recalling the redness of the bright star, happiness and
revolutionary fervour:

It can stay perfect as long as it is not exposed.

*

Do you think this conception of politics takes into account *any* structural relations, moves in *any way* beyond iconography? The part played by labour in the transition.
Imbue anything you see with dreams. We cannot escape fantasy.

Style is mere endurance.
There is all order, and beauty, luxury, peace and pleasure.
Luxury and voluptuousness. Beauty is a kind of order,
a kinder order, sufficient in itself, its own stability.
*This strategy sounds suspiciously like the programme of the counterrevolutionary party of the parliamentary bourgeoisie in the Second Empire.*

*

Music is absolute privacy. What it has become. Was it good
    for you too?
You wake up and your dream falls flat, you wake up and
    your dream comes true,
you wake up and someone says, was it good for you too. I
really wish that people didn't act the way they do. Music is a
    monument to a metaphor we live by. Any metaphor.
ANY object, divisible into ANY number of parts, I appreciate
ANY kind of information.

Music is absolute lunacy.

*

The memory was the screen and the sky of disaster.

Experiencing ourselves in a thousand fragments,
doing everything that will make a good life a dream come true,
the spirit level dies inside our accumulated doubt,
the smashed-up fragments of political clout.

You should join up in revolution against the middle classes.
The artefacts of the rich must be appropriated for whatever
    use we can make of them.
The theatre, the instruments & all the costumes will be burnt.
Human knowledge and the building up of culture is an immortal
    quest.
To fulfil it you have to break it.
Tear it to pieces.
Knowing when to move, when to wait.

*

The song rises again,
You LIVE and you LEARN, you get
BORN and you DIE. The wind moves
when I wave my hands.
Open up the vault and all the light
will come shining through.


Waves breaking as bodies breaking, in the far distance,
Across some object called the sea.

# THE PROBLEM, THE QUESTIONS, THE POEM (PART I)

*So going on with my trade one whit and gardenin, and riding another I rit downe these questions following.*

*What is the cause we dreame of things wee never saw, or knew, or even heard of.*

## ( O N E )

## THE POEM

How does it lie. Does it memorialize or anticipate. Progress. Regress. Protest. Captivate. Dissipate. Fluctuate. Masturbate.

I wrote the first poem the day after the day of love, on the day of love's official registration, to mark it well. Each poem mourns the other poems, the other people, their other selves left behind inside itself, and it brings them back to life inside itself, eating them up to become them. Only what's said is said, and therefore alive. Mortal words breathe and die, the ordering of an anticipated not-real reality that nonetheless—in the mental sphere, and written, and spoken—assumes reality.

These things dance around inside and come spinning out outside of me, on everyone's wrong side. Everything is blind. We all can see as far as any of our eyes can see, we can help each other know the things that are most enclosed in privacy, the things we do not even let ourselves begin to admit to begin.

Here is the creature or creator as a self-dramatized idea of an idea of self, in no one's waking dream. Doing it wrong again and again, I say all this but really I want to know what love might mean. These things mean: that Rachmaninov's hands were so big they could take and hold anything. His music had all the feeling it was possible to have and can we make it the basis for having more, in touch capaciously, believing with all sincerity in every switch in harmony, in every big tune. You can only say that these things are ironically true to you, true to life.

The defence façade corroded.

Order is restored and the universe is off piste. In peace. We
are resting in peace.
You speak with such
fetching false
teeth.

It dies. What dies.
Goodbye. Hello.

Here it all lives again.

Sign or consign, co-sign, witness my will though you can't see
        the script;
between two persons, in two minds, the straight face reversed
in statement says, I don't want to complete anything, but you
        are there,
so to speak,
        in speech,
and we did, speak, but of that substance nothing only vague
intimation remains, of such intimacy
that once was all the world.

Then the music of Ravel on the radio is pure melancholy, as I
explain it comically, hyperbolically, the filtration of loss and
desire through the decadent restraint of nostalgia for what
never was, calmly in tune. But also at times it is catastrophe,
crescendo till it explodes.

Accused of a nihilistic will-to-destructive-being-towards death,
at the end of a civilization or a particular mode of highly
developed society, within the highest and most developed
forms of that mode, exaggerating their contradictions, with all
the thrill and the sadness of breakage and loss.

Speak to me, it speaks to me, in the kitchen, on the floor, getting up and going on out of that door.

The world is not a symphony, is not in sympathy, binds up its ears with the waxen image of something too perfect to be moulded around and upon.

Frustrated that you got this all wrong, were not tempted to extend address in a way they could see other people among that thus dressed up to be words, architecture, each building building itself up and tearing itself down.


Drunk with drink or love, imagining that any of this is interesting,

Getting down off the ladder, I step up. I step up. Or, up, I step down, lounge around, growl I am hungry for more. The throat clears and it begins to speak in rhyme and the line extends as far as the eye can descry or describe the horizon that opens up and closes in. Everything and something, no one and nothing, you, me or we are all breaking and making, slipping and slipping up. After all, anyone could say anything, but who are you to say?

A whole mass of people have a universal claim on the gold rushing from the chopped neck of the god heedlessly rushing to the gate eager hands are tearing down.

Lying on the ground the grass gets thinner, greener, or better, depending on the weather. On the water, sheaves, the water flows, the leaves, with renewed hope for the future fracked from the sky itself.

My eye is as far from me as the sea is a hopeless anomaly that will swallow us all alive.

My knee bends and cracks at the hip, my waist repeats all the mistakes the human frame tells a story about itself, to itself, and hangs on the frames, formatting it in an institution tells it where to go, what to do.

Think for yourself, make your own mind up of books, and air, and occasional activities such as the practice of activist networks and occasional spectacular events rejuvenating the soul and then retreated back into healing or making a thing of being sick, taking it all in.

The problem is that the subject seeks to self-abnegate by eating everything up, and eaten away from inside decides to decry itself with the sighs of its self-abolishing re-affirmation, sneaking in the big back door. I want to tell you all, *ALL OF YOU*, why I am here and everything is so near we can touch and taste the rainbow making our differences a smiling example that shines the world over in a broadly HD beam. When I say me I mean the world, and none other than myself.

Do you really want to know everything that 'love' could really mean. That love. And saying that you do, do you really want to know what the figuration and configuration of the really approaching end of any world as a framework as a living dream means, seen in movies as scenes that any number of actors could be the voices and the friends swallowed in something that seems so small and so very far away in each tiny bar of each tiny heart whispering assessment in each tiny room paid and not paid for. Someone else has struggled for each word you speak.

I'll be travelling on my own.

# THE PROBLEM

The problem is that the subject swallows up all those other voices and sources—conversations, with friends, at parties, on the bench, on the train, in the middle of the night shaking with rage and the social milieu you're in; or historical accounts, bits of the poems that swirl in the head, living with them very deep in the bed of the brain shaping a conscious or unconscious thought, theoretical frameworks invoked as parodic half-digested bulwarks of argument, of what has and might have been taught—that the subject swallows and spits them out to claim them, as *its own* self-multitude, containing contradiction;

which is also part of the process of turning on itself, in disgust at its having an emotional life at all, as the self-obsession with the nuanced ordinary feeling of a 'bourgeois individualism'; which is also falsely mapped onto and elided with a self-disgust at the poet's positioning in the middle of the class road, which also keeps turning on others with snide asides and half-references or détournements of things people have said, in and out of poetry; which comes to seem antagonistic polemic, shooting off, yet one without a fixed position; so that these two poses— polemical certainty, however parodied as academic jargon or nonsensical or nihilistic sloganeering, being against all organic life, and constant self-mocking contradiction are not *generous*, are not satisfying—this conflict is not the *reader's*, is not *given* to them, is not *open* enough to them. The use of the second person pronoun is often a part of this, functioning often as a non-differentiated or un-specified object of seeming, even if that attack and that address is self-directed. The poems can't work out whether rhyme is a mellifluous flow of pleasurable affect or a stupid tool of satire. The short lyric poems would seem to be more comfortable with the former, but get barraged, when they do appear in flashes in the larger whole. This has also to do with length of line.

## THE QUESTIONS

The sun comes down from such giddy heights each day, it needs to relax.

Why are there fireworks in the sky?

Why are there still fireworks in the sky?

At the party talking about guilt and shame, were you feeling shame and guilt?

## THE POEM

Not on the run but counting the exits and the ways. Not letting anyone block the door. Whether you choose to open up or to shut down possibility, trapped inside the house, trapped *outside* the house with no way back or no way in, is calmness more interesting than alarm.

Another new day is a wide band spanning the possibility of recalled tranquil action, trees that fall like tears that fall like trees that root the sense of renewal in watered grief.

It was so bad.

Someone said something was like something else, or someone was like someone else, some thing like some one like each step back went to the routed square paced in amplification widening down.

Why is it the *road* that you take, the metaphor of travel, of travail, why did I ever go away or not stay awake with the body at my side. A distance had opened up in the clasp of a dead arm in sleep, who could say what was there within the face shut wide open to rest, to the rest, to the world enclosed and clasped together by ourselves away from. Narrative vicissitude and clarity, each pole-axed polarity, each invested hope makes no return as hope but cannot be—in another sense—anything *other* than just re-enacted return. Every little thing you do.

Map the paths, map the sun, whatever it is you find yourself guided to. The sea is hungry, the sea is wanting, say swallows that swallow up some idea displaced onto them, even the idea of outside itself, objects that fly past but stay stone-frozen, the things that died, quick movement as the tale buoys it up, trails off.

Come clean into it, cold.

A sound of waves is heard.

Who hears, who reveals, baked in sweat or dying of any ill in the coldest winter yet.

Fifty pages of poems and the entirety of life make a big size scowl or sneer at the fact or idea of wanting queer displacement in the cage. Not wanting to talk, or to talk too much, to open up the hutch and let the little domestic animals of childhood, the first thing you remember that you owned, run amok all over your protecting heart. Open the throat. Do you count the times you are struck by the possibility of death each day or is this just the play of a child who remembered non-existence for the first time and in that thought just stayed there giving up. Without a sibling share, over-share, abundant spilling, it all goes out but then comes back in. No feeling is greater than the re-entry into the blood. I wrote my doctor a letter to the government to the private care espoused and being lost each day.

You now understand the *condition* of what it is to be a *woman*. Rivulets trickle into the sea. The waters evaporate.

For the earth as a whole is warm.

Ask each object what it is. It asks or answers back. The idea of a screen onto which images are projected is the technological fact of a life known through the films with which we make our pact, with what the medium *itself* desires.

In our lives we keep a little mystery. Did you ever think about leaving me. Something or someone is gone. It is the poem's lost un-recaptured tone. It anticipates its going, pleasures in each tooth that falls into the mother's lost pot. Does father punch the face. It is getting hot. My wedding dress, my bridal gown, my clothing's covering in feathered down. Dis-robe, de-press, wake up and go naked yet. I so much love you like you. That would be kind.

Like like and unlike lacks the wit to charm the birds into the hand outstretched and circling the coastal breach erodes. What walls will fall once everything in my head explodes. Silly to be in the condition of hurt but not blessed, a walking wound makes you, what, the walking dead? Save I know I ever only saw one corpse once, I saw each flap of skin of one I did not know taken off, as if in a dream, the face, as of personality and humanity itself, gently professionally and carefully scraped and then thrown off. Each mask that helps one to see.

But this is real. *You* are. Are you

O private personhood, wherever
ever
have you gone, press-ganged to go away, to sail all seven sides
of a world-discovering life. I find a world in other people that
are globally within the destruction through death of a law I
hate to need. It is so beautiful to think of the raising of the
dead even now among us, they saw them on the road, invented
hallucinatory power and through this we learn to love to
live and put away childish things, syllables, keep, hold. The
question is missing. The question mark. Enter, back.

## THE PROBLEM

The problem is the problem, to find out how to be a poet.
Accessible parking, wet floor. What you need to know. I can
bring my own. The legs are spread. Hearing bands on a march,
marchers as bands, do we sing, do we hold hands. For reduced
filth. Flush. Flesh. Delight! Charm will magic everything into
being wonderful and we can own it each our separate selves
extended not the other who made it, listening at the rapping
table not a worker but a ghost, a greater personage, cares so
much for the self, strokes the surface, even. All the daughters
or the sons I will never have called Ezekiel, make the valley
heave up its bones to a life I will never lead and

The object that provoked the poem is carefully re-worked,
re-moved, relieved. The stimulus becomes another field of
things that handily are there, they are too easily seen.

Truly the simplest, what's wrong.
It comes out of the tap hot. My bag is open, is it /
broken. Visitors get shown around. My heart is open, is it

You can normally enter through there.

# THE QUESTIONS

Ease of life, ease of craft. Try too hard.

Of these things enough has been spoken, has enough been read, what token falls flimsily beneath its wish to reach, its reach to wish the matter in hand. Is friendship enough. Wan and won.

Where are the snows of yester-year, built up as drift?

Who is it falls down the cracks of each successive rift?

Who deserves their making into some other person's proffered gift?

Said no to, say on.

## ( T W O )

## THE POEM

Twice I dreamed of you, as spring.

Moving up and down the coast, we have the whole summer.

I would like to have them, the seasons, all of them, cutting down every living thing, launch an all-out attack in UK English, protracted and split up, unnecessary stress—material —natural—we would talk it over, done talking over, the bad time happens hard.

Lift up your heels, on adventure holidays getting away you don't find out who you are, or what you are, your message awaiting approval, maybe nothing in escaping.

In the streets, the blood, how could you do this? The flowers, the smell, you,
escaping
folded
goaded
golden heart.

It seems so far back. I can see it. In myth, in legend, the puns on the fairies, in their secrets give up, that basically what means the world,

is no big deal, it gently wins, extinction forms, worked in their minds.

With great bitterness I say it dies in peak and ordinary peak, trails off as speech. Death is so small, unkind. The least orgasm.

Disappoint.

No looking back is personal, memory here is figured as the impersonal, when the personal comes in the community will collapse. It is so hard to have built up so much of your sense of self on a gradated sense of fine and even coarsely woven feelings, only to have the tapestry catch fire in the light of specific ignited incidents which demand objective response, it is so hard, I loved them.

In love it looks sad.

He dressed their wound and loved them. In private places. The father for his children, loves them, but public embraces are hard and remain merely as shallow traces. Something in the nature of daily life, when you get out of the theatre it is still the theatre but it is no longer, dark, and magical, the light is so bright at first it hurts your eyes and then it is the same scene you saw on-going going on. But changed? Here it would be easy to bring music in and to say,

Transposition, the problem of each new thing offered in clusters exceeds the bounds of the previous thing that had been. Each day learning something new about us, about me, about you. It is a not a good thing. The same mistakes repay the same pay-offs, the commune flops, each group goes mentally wound-up and the structures are not in place to tame the gendered force of harm. But harm makes it too passive, too hurtfully inward, a person does something, a group, dominating the group. If we can't even do it in our utopia here, fostered and cheered in a thousand forum formulations, a thousand reading-groups, in horizontal spread or the closed top ranks of even the small inflated party, where then can we do it, *can* it be done?

# THE PROBLEM

The problem is the problem that I am wearing a T-Shirt because it is warm and I like the warm feeling on my arms.

I wrote hearts for hurts.

Writing and reading in the sun.

To recapitulate: is all that can be offered in the place of these individual instantiations of continuing injustices, imbalances, without consent, each bad iota of tacit, implicit and actual force, to convey and inhabit the habit of being within the condition of a certain kind of convivial pleasure, an open, capacious expansiveness, everything that is not boring and gives pleasure and charm, everything that seems not to try to bring harm?

Or, on the other hand, to match the violence, accelerate and in berating have the same feeling reversed?

Of a hate that says on the basis of love it must hate. Non-violence objectively not passion a hex, a curse, evisceration, a list, murder, a purpose, clean, a stab, a grab in despair for the most extreme thing.

What does this mean it makes us do, or not do?

Enough, or too much?

Too much, or too little?

Not near, not nearly.

What is held the closest to us, can we ever let it go?

# THE POEM

Dear.

Some of the things in this poem are the most personal thing.

The quotations direct.

I pressed not the lighter but the cigarette onto my face with
an eager to please please a stranger, dressed as a stranger, I
had no way of knowing. I burned off my own face, singed, a
scar. Every bad thing in me. There is not a finger I cannot lift.
Burning burning burning, burning burning
burning.

These people are separate.

What does he really think about the aristocracy?

What feelings does he have about these things in the world,
these things not invoked but observed?

How much do you think in holding back you lose, how
much protect, at what cost protect, waiting for surprise to
be no more pleasant than hurt, disguised, pleasure, boredom,
trauma? Can you be troubled by reckoning them all the same,
what the mode you adopted had made you say? But too much
troubled, too much in love, too much alarm raises the roof or
brings it down so hard the head cannot breathe and be more
than fermented itself.

When we spoke our great debate by the man in the back seat
of the bus, he was amused, how much disturbed, with great
violence HEGEL and you were wearing a serious shirt. I stood

outside while you ate.

It is this moment in that I have been coming back to, the moment before the waltz restarts, when with complete abandon to the discipline of that form the decision to go in, again, to launch even further to its heights its ultimate limit the spirit that lay within it, so violent the elegance of our time. I will come and find you, it says, besides and outside yourself. Together it is that we know we both are lost and lost forever, o my darling form, in me you must know the end of my self. The poem does not end. It does not end here, the laughing bastards sneer, the universal task, encourage *each* and *every* branch of mental, of physical, intellectual and spiritual activity, if we are to accomplish this what goal our
goal, of universal love.

## THE PROBLEM

The problem is that it is with some playfulness, where are you going, do you even have to say why or how? Where, for you, is here?

Pain leads into life but once gone it remains, life, without weight, as if no solid thing. But the pain, too, was not solid, but known, and then turned solid, invested fetish the turn from *quality*, as such, but what then was quality in itself but already metaphorically displacement of the same kind as any other kind of figuring extreme.

It *is, so much,* your face.

The centre exploded to the extremities of life. What fields had been passed. It is the passive in the voice that removes, and this may be a necessary removal, but what removal from life goes too far from what made life, life, and worth, living up to what claim for it it could even have been said it had made or been made to make itself.

But really what you are talking about is people.

But really what you are talking about are structures.

But really what you are talking about is the talking itself, finding out there, not really knowledge you can put back on the shelf, the appearance of thinking that gives itself up as a ghost in that shell too early, content without a centre really to be that shell, it is so pretty and cleaned of the muck and shit outside, in the rain, over a sustained period of time, placed by the foot and by the door. Vomit-covered objects in the box. To look at your stool. Says ultimate solipsism in the dung-heap.

Others as sequences, people felt differently,
others as forms, people felt themselves to be figured themselves differently,
the gorgeous unknown, still unknown and to be gorgeous, just that, the fabulous the idea of that made cheaply manifest, the histories that go on in the voices inside ourselves, without even having to be seen as histories, even to be known, when we know what it is we tell ourself.

How much accepting of imperfection.

Is the quality *by definition* restlessness, restlessness in itself?

Who ever means love.

# THE QUESTIONS, THE POEM

The questions become the poem, the problem.
The problem becomes the solution becomes the problem again.

Some thing, some time. The poem does not end.

Sickness in movement, on boats and rivers, on trains. Going
away. As health.

Where does the light come from? They look like they have
interior light.

Is this outside? Coming back to it, worked and reworked, not
to turn back, as condition for progress, fell by the side of the
road. And again the hungry sea.

Take out the names. Where does anyone go, in time or in
space, what does forward mean in some onward building
drive?

Take out the names.

*You* end.

The poem does not end.

## ( THREE )

## THE POEM

Children disguised as ignorance,
The trill disguised as love,
love turns weird, in odd scalar combinations and the recurrence
on the skittered staccato hop half-mocked it sings, or left
pleased in calm the distance across the triangle contact in some
contract drawn with whoever listens, impossible not to write
blithe, dignified, and with a sad cadence fall when at first all
alone it sings its song, the voice you did not even recognize
as your own. Explaining painting from a valuable stupidity,
enthusiastic perception and thought to be lived for the rest of
a life digested in colour and shape melding and moulding as
clarity and confusion in these halls.

Technique.

Wonderful, wonderful times.

The swoon, the slur, the smear, gross, too lop-sided, too
small. Deep. Too quiet.
Too loud.

I have been thinking about this, it was not just Rachmaninov's
hands but his heart, you can hear it in the music. To say so is
so easily stupid. They were *huge*!

But Ravel's face on the cover in the leaves *was* too small, his
features too hard to scrutinize, his eyes. What face? I have
looked at this face for hours. Its every feature, its last. Things
about the hair. What is the first thing that dies, what touch,
how close? What store of universal truths?

Neo-classicism known for no real classical order, no real holding back of the chaos in each instance of the most measured measure, unbearably serene.

And then this re-surge or up-surge which *knows* its extreme and holds it in, before bursting as it were the day would burst and surprise itself by bursting, hold back, no hole, barred, borne back. The metaphor here would be *going up*, which means you must come down, you cannot live there. Is it catharsis, is it will to death or life, is it *anything* like any real-life love you had?

My shirt, my shirt. My shoes.

Juliet is the sun, is false, is nonsensical, is a statement, that she makes the day and that she gets up each morning, rarely defended. Is it living or is it dead – how can something be both a creation and a discovery? Each thing like another thing.

My heart.

The mirror we make of a world in the face.

To start off with it was dark.

The conversation could be infinitely extended, each topic touched around or on giving way with easy flow. Sitting and wishing you could look at the clouds, the trails of condensation air stretched umbrellas in white on blue, skimming the tops of trees in dream, giddy and breathless, a little sad too. I will become this sex, a straw, melting in the ice, a hand beside. Laid aside.

# THE PROBLEM

In lyric the unknown fullness of a future deferred, a debt incurred, provisional in the future who are you. Whether echo or stop. I rhymes with who. Resonate. To exclude memory and desire. Impossible, impassable, gripped in fear.

In lyric hope who writes the future, for those who can barely *live* in the present, in it or *below* it, its task. Falling into it, organizing the surrounding day, as love, which never will break.

The more you said it wasn't for you, the more they believe it was *all* for you. The door keeps slamming shut. Each report is like a shot.

*Our nature. My greatest privacy.*

# THE QUESTIONS

The first questions I went and found in a corner, in a case, in a tower, in a building, in a book, the least happiness and physical curiosity, the most pleasure in the world, *giving* pleasure and taking and laughing quietly, for hours, by a wall.

There is nothing antique about it.

If I have had the most pleasure in the world.

If we can say this is the worst, it is not the worst. The least.

There is nothing antique about it.

Like the sea, but *not* like the sea.

It is not disembodied, it is *you*.

The sound of ripping outside. Is this too direct, or is this too indirect?

Will you *ever* let me back in? Will the poem? Where is love?

## THE POEM

The best. Very erotic. All that repetitive dynamism. When I started to get all excited, I started to dance. Hold your breath, do you dare. Closeness costs lives. In shade from sun to die and hide, respite holds tight the night is wide; What was Eden on the bench, where the dream did nightly end, what was sleep in the streets and trees, the empty cars, the knees that bruise and fall, the tongues that lock, the knocking teeth.

Someone put something else in.

Is doubt motion, motion doubt? The dislocation provoked by care, devotion.

These are the breaks. This is a public face. Flight or masquerade. Seeking a language more livid than vomit, the beautiful scrawl of tender anonymous love on the toilet wall, the act of love, physical, in a number and a name connected to no one yet known, in imagination play raised in public lost within.

Each go their separate ways, depart. The feeling, still, of still being forced to co-habit there, by force of habit, where habitually the move away from the mind or the bonds of a more sustained sociality sees love pitched in the place of shit.

The palace.

Falling asleep in the flesh you wake up when a knock at the door interrupts the thought of all possible paradises entertained in vision you could scarcely believe or remember you had entertained.

One tune falls into another. Afford no advantage to the description of order, the ghost of a rose not smelled in sleep, to dream of paradise itself, when sleep itself must end. Buried in language. Can you see through the hands that cover your eyes, handsome wounds of the flesh, can you see through the eyes that cover your hands. Things in touching distance come closer, part, then pass.

Weather as metaphor. Sky. Masses of water and land.

Words as raw material that, as it were, would, created, last forever in transformed communication.

It was about to be realized on earth.

In another instance the melody seems to begin to proffer comfort, but then becomes yearning at the turning from the possibility of that comfort's promised fulfilment, denied, self-denied. This turning inclines both to and away from love as too much a united cost to bear, to have to learn to live with, preferring to deal in a slow sad comfort that is the prevention of the original idea of comfort itself, constituting *that very idea*.

The burial of urns.

Every good thing goes away. I want to read everything there is about this, to know everything I can. Fixed to this area, removed. The birds sing, no one knows what they are singing but we can make it anything we want. You can only have anything. There has to have been an occasion but its origins are of necessity lost, erased, faded but present in every single trace. There may have been occasion, noble and sentimental now waving your arms without hands in the air, without a strong enough opposable thumb to press and make fire emerge from the aperture there.

How to be human. The gate. The history of the universe.

How many things you can describe as beautiful.
How to go on. How it goes on.

## THE PROBLEM, THE QUESTIONS, THE POEM

But your heart is pounding.

We must all be so sentimental.

Turning footnotes to endnotes,
You will not say what it is.

Why the wind makes such a noise and is not seen. Why one is not like another.
What is called love.

No one can ever see the sky all of the time, and no one ever sees all of the sky.

Each year, where are the snows, etc. Each day.

I have that line in my head each day.

How to be human. What to do. I always get that one wrong.

Does it get hard to breathe. Do you forget to. Extension, forward, in the back, breathing into each other's mouths the breathing gets hard and they must part, lovers in order to breathe or to escape the possibility of, breathing, never really being able to breathe, never being able to say you have had air, the mirror to the mouth mists to prove a life, still a strong beat in the places you could put your fingers to. If you stretch very far, how far or how much you can see, remembering the high voice you never lose, switching between the ways of being you told yourself to form. Useless I want you, recognized, judged, perceived. Useless want more, want how, know nonetheless

The poem is each object you lose and collect, re-shuffled in the cabinet with extra shelves, but the glass is broken, your selves, do they get out, how do they get out, how did they all get out, suffocating.

*Malevolence*, if it must be named.

The floor. The wall.

The window. The door.

The rise. The fall.

The bottom. The top.

The space. The clock. The side.

The sky. The sea.

A tree. A star.

A scar.


People think you can do things.

# AESTHETICS OF RESISTANCE
## *FOR FRANCES KRUK*

Could adequate monstrous
Destruction be dreamed,
      Monstrous form,
The fires our eyes, of the Same
Size but
changed to a bundle,
      the day broken
Wide, when recorded in an
Inventory
When Recorded
In an Inventory,
In that image burning whole.


      When recorded in
      an Inventory,
      At this point, a distinct group
forms as ugly and ridiculous,
Changed to a pitcher,
Changed to a young boar.

The flames added in the sky,
These flames were turned to blue:
You see changed to a bundle,
      Changed to a bundle,
Changed to an array of hams and cheeses,
Overpainted with a simple decoration.
Changed to a calf. One of the few
That has not been changed.
Changed to a goose

or swan. Changed to livestock.
The shadow in the over-painted
areas, can be seen.


      Could it be
      Dreamed, could it be
      Thought, fought for
These, for the Cast
Out We hold
But cannot hold close
Enough to see
      In the clear
      Attained meaning
      The storm.


They came
      We listened
Were not
Listened
      To


We thirsty mouths
Howl Sorry we are
So Hungry
These breaths rattle
      open Doors Chairs
      Chains Whispers
      laced Latched tight
      Collapsible
      Chairs legs
      Without Seating
      In the losing

Game:

On the last note the last left
Falling.


      Picked up,
The story gets Fleshed
out
        What it's taken
To build up
          The bones of the body
I call my own
          What each one
          Gets made of
In the flesh
          Sold to eat
          And lift and Settle
Down:

          Is a life
          Is so called.


      It is a Pause
A space a
Point A tiny ope-
          ration of Thought
All the tiny spiders
Crawling the mines the
  little Normal Cracks the
Small Dead
of History
In the forest Basement

clinging
   in the
Flash See in
      for dear life See
  Chasm
Spark


They knock
     We answer
Back: sur
     Vive. Fuck death
and fuck
     What is not life
what Cannot make
     Provision
Lived to flourish
     Fuck the cruelty
That Normal narrows down
     Fuck what pre-
Vents un
     Encumbered breath

FOR LECTURES
*IN MEMORIAM*
*STEPHEN RODEFER*

**1.**

I swear to GOD
with everyone
who sure makes a lot of noise
and I say all his lines
and I say them wrong:
would take them away
would speak them out aslant.

As this corner is brilliant
it must be rounded
vaulted Over-
turned.

**2.**

Tune up. This now *really* gets
going. You could call it
the last great stage play—
the great chain—transplant
to what gets paltry dumbed
to job applicant supplicant
parade.

For each notch off
of crude loaf, not at ease to observe,
with much chomping dulled,
to be called a 'verse'—
So *very* much disinclined but
Speak up!

## 3.

Ow. Which means ouch.
And in some other languages
some different things. Please
don't do that again.

You burned Paris. Whose turn now.
Thelonious Monk plays a piano
with his left hand and a celeste
with his right. What is outside
almost drowns it out Even so we listen
on. In lines deformed and half-
remembered, since its initial and
controversial burst, we have not been
sought out, have not sought respite.
It is for sure not an anthem
and for sure it is not trite.

**4.**

Our attendants have all gone,
But now is not a time to wait;
When I heard the news
What I'd just packed away,
each thing *deformed into another*,

What is the colour beneath
the cover, includes as it isolates,
shows through. Visible a secret history,
*scraped on, if not away :*
The music in painting; The
painting in music; Poetry in
spite of everything.

*We'll all go and be exiles*
o lectern
give me strength
doing nothing but to read, assist
insistent horrible brothers
with whom we spend our time:
temporarily embarrassed millionaires
betrayed, who are gathered
and known.

**5.**

*This* is not the business of poetry
let me plant no other tree
than this one, this
with its withered
hardened centre yet
Yet it spreads—
      To SPROUT;
            To STAND and SING:
And it I cannot slay.

How soon is soon
When all that's disappeared
sums up stunned

What's left is
a complex replacement the same
concentrated where together apart,
some you love, leave,
live in new      strictures of circumstance
*deliberately decomposed ,*
running under, unseen.

**6.**

This starts on a high note
where even we
Have never been.

*And again I say*
Give voice, to lend
when nothing is left,
*an alternative version*
*which both resists and embodies,*
miserable it's true:

How are you
Doing, how
Getting on by:
the same.

**7.**

Well then get up the cliff and pull it down with you;
Get up the mountain top whichever
wrong way up: what use to make
these chippings from the block.

Tell us what you saw up there
Tell us what you saw
for I was blind but now I read
with furious scratching fist
scrawled in clamp
all balled up to write

As he disappeared into the mist
the mountains And never came back
except every time
like a stage direction, difficult and strange,
will translate to cause
then all at once in two times that speak:
In two tongues:
you yours, and I, mine,
spooling most tainted and unabashed
in parks, in parking lost
for a moment to reside
swung round
wherever would crack a chorus out
of all sorts
in harmony below:

What the clouds thought they were
to be read
got down
 at dawn.

**8.**

It is them we defy
no *more mild*
than any time:

Than this:
flexed crippled
double-joint
broken joist
how's the prison population how's
it well holding up
the labour pool What
new thing to foist
on poetry, necessary and dumb.

So this is
its theme:
Of poetry as necessity
of thee I sing
This desk is filth
My room a mess
Set your stanzas in order

Economies of words
self-locking
what could not be released
except all at once you did get to be able to do it
recto and reverso
we'll steal them all.

**9.**

And always
it is in opposition
as you experienced it well enough
would *prefer*, would *demand*
no less than NINETY, twelve
tones will not suffice

Boom. But your call
to say the name
in a factory to the spheres
where I'm just a poor
loveable gaping gasping break

So don't you ever stop
streaked to nothing less than
the stars
attuned

Humming
what once was brilliant
as the fire it's come from and the wing it flies
to the future not consumed.

**10.**

You have come from here
a place in many texts
whose names are not marked
but manifest
as big as a city and deep.

Then in naming them will we break
down these artefacts
stations of the retro
not hardly
lingered
for what skips a beat
then redoubles
sounding plain though muffled a while
in caverns of the art
as this is any one artist's fantasy
to *SURRENDER* and *SURVIVE*,
SHIFT and MELD.

*There is no way now that it can be*
*anything but apocalyptic;*
*The word itself sounds the*
*end*, as in language it drives the
blood. I'm still here:
But *LOOK* : but *LISTEN UP* :

*The man we're looking for is gone.*

# FROM SAPPHO AND RILKE

# MORNING SONG

## [1]

If I can be
      up
      at crack,
I'll part the
      morning
      tide.

My morning
mouth
      disfigured
and hideous
      it opens
to speak:

All who died
for this
say yes,
      get up
off
your feathered
bed get
      down,
check your bad
self as it flowers,
      take up
your head
floating singing
river run.

This contraband

is song so smuggled
snug. It flows undone.

And WHAT, on EARTH
or Heaven best
ignored, do we
*want it to do?*

# [2]

SAPPHO be kind.
ORPHEUS and angels
          with back
to storm drive on
          to smash
your mouth.


          O
so
          fucked up.

Orphans mine.

Sappho sang
and the chariot immense
was pulled on the smallest
of wings. One
               more
          lost
               plane.

The final reams
          fragment,
          the wreck
be smoking yet.

The arc as it curves,
          bends back—
all at sea in flight,
wings singed indifferent by the sun.

Then what remains: as ash

it burns a blackened line,
                    to write:


Sappho in love sang
of the love of Women
              for no Man
she excluded correct
and the CHARIOT was
pulled the FATHER
dumbfound
And Sappho sang.

Orpheus by women
              was torn.

# [3]

RATION your language.
Rein in.
It is not for the eating.
                    SPEAK
to the bird and pray
to GOD you are next
to be eaten up.


Word is not responding.
A bird's heart stops beating
in the mine. We will keep on
digging. This heart is mine,
I mean it, can you see it
on my arm unsleeved and
bleeding. Yet the underground
has come to pass.
        We blink
                in light.
Mountains to molehills, cut down
                            to size.

> *O love, we are not like*
> *birds together, are not*
> *of one mind. The empty*
> *trees are dead inside.*
> *What was this landscape*
> *of love to fly.*

# AUTUMN DAY
### *After Rilke*

*Where are you*, ancient
                    September,
the truck slips on the road
and I cannot even
                    drive:
*Of course*
          I'm lost
this autumn day
O lord it's time.

Summer was too big to fail
so now fall down
the first fruits last,
ripeness is
naught. So let us
drink the heavy wine.

The lost drop we'll squeeze
will drink them dry.

Who has no house has no hope left.
Who has no love will no love find.
So up all night, to read, to correspond,
each street to pace it up and down;
without rest, surcease, when
                              in
                              leaves
                              the
                              pages
                of my book
                to spine will bind
My dumb and broken back.

# FIRST ELEGY
*After Rilke*

Of ornament
I have my store—yet still
                I ask:
Where, when I scree
                would be
                ordained
                to fall.

And then
I ask
        Who on heaven
        on EARTH would
                hear me;
of animal, vegetable, mineral
kingdoms, what dominion
                and what
                rank
        in all the dumb halls
                of HEAVEN
        would lend an ear.

For truly beauty
        is the beginning of
terror, the base is born in blood.

Not to destroy me
        for this I revere
am clutched so strong.
Imagine springtime
        needs you
emptiness quivers in

rapture
        Yet
Punished in
Coitus for
        intimacy together
we break and broach
        exchange.


All systems
        go on. The women
men trade.


As for me,
        Books replace my love.
How in whose Name
can I sing her
        when she is not here,
how sing him,
                when he is.


Who you are is
again in the poem a trope.
To sing in state
of fugue. The other voice
is not heard, does it not exist
deep down to grow;
will rot at root.


Within the ear so tall
and sudden rose,
Not lovely as a tree
        is gnarled
        and poetry,
better than all God's creation,

will spread to green
inside. This meadow rots my heart.
That place is all fenced off.

And so, citizen or not, I declare
My country is poetry,
it borders
        on control;
Aphrodite
        who daily
        I petition
to steel my arm
        to arm my heart
        to lend me voice
in stead
        to write these lines.

# ENVOY

It is autumn.
We soldier on.
My love I cannot
stop, my love once
       started
It is not like a tap
       turned off.

So Sappho threw herself
       from the rocks.
Immortalize. Across
my heart the tracts
of love,
       they beat
           my life,
       it cannot
           be sent.

       Can it be tracked.

O you would wish death
in a rush and in a wave.

But down to size,
positions that you try,
in fantasy confused:
These versions are to
       change in time.
As texts they do
       remain.
           Reader
What follows

for your own use,
on your own head
the fitting cap
if it be fitted right.

So pick up your pen
and write.
We hope that you
are satisfied.

# SAPPHO

## [1]

Once I threw a Gauntlet Down,
                     Once, Goaded Desire,
from the Rock a Beacon a Far a
                             Flame.

But now, the end In sacred word Is silent sounded
on the head of all this land. From this
silence we may infer. Re-
member the time:

       Once more I dive, once more take off
       my body this song on air bent
       down
       and drunk
           with love.

Not sacred but we must bring it down. From each
extreme. Some nights I think that O
                                 I
would be as mad
as all the sane not willing not
giving over all
the one-eyed herds disguised
seeing double to drive
in exchange for
               just
               one drop
               of dark, red wine;
               one single cup, wine-dark
                     to throw from the high

                                        white
                                        rock
              my self, this body execrable
                              in offering
                              to the wine-
                                        dark
                                        brine:

Having no word for what colour of the sea
is named as blue: a mere reflecting,
                              dark, or lighter,
                                        lower, or higher
as the sky or the cup in its passions transform
O transform us, save or destroy
what's not conceived in our too-ready structuring:

Intoxicated, eyebrows arched in mild surprise,
relaxed. Unhappy when drunk is a crazy one,
when it raises excitement high exchange,
to touch my limb your heart we opened in re-
membered meadow bed already made.

                      And then dancing and
                              forgetting
root of the river out of mind
in death forever with no
more mortal dread.

It is luxury I love and this,
the lust for sun, has won
all brightness and beautiful
shimmering charade.

Don't settle for less.

*Not SAPPHO, but SERCO*
and all entwined;
    Of this
    so sing,
        beyond a-
            genda'd desire.

But oblivion is no way to go.

# [2]

This prayer send up I Expedite
to one on throne embossed—
Father's Child, weaver of wiles,
don't go crushing my heart.

With application made, with form
filled in, to you as one divine I plead:
Return if ever once you heard,
   leaving Father's house,
   swift sparrows the chariot
Depart: to listen to my bleeding:
   *in every part I am bleeding:*
   you'll ask: what was it this time?

What specific explicit request
from frenzied heart's desire.
What form will fit. Is it the
right one. If you fail you'll
never get it back.

To soothe you said
What's refused will be given I
   asked please
release me from gruel and grind
fill *up* at last my *longing* heart. As allies
in this war.

No apparatus of state so proudly
armed so rudely forc'd
is fair but the beloved is my sole
request. It's so transparently
clear: so easily seduced

from family home, so easily
bent...and nimbly...I remember
the one not here, would prefer
their lovely walk the radiance
        on their face

        than all the arms of men.

        O take your gifts away.

Because of this at once I look
and cannot speak
with frozen tongue and epidermic
flame. Blind and deaf, will no longer
sing a quiet verse, and I am greener
                        than grass,
death's little bit

        cut down to size
        these words I'm biting back.

## [3]

But I will try to sing this hymn
      just one more time:
come now luxuriate in grace
which means not all selected;
is not demand enough; still
            *someone* will remember us
                  *someone* must
as beautifully for my companions
                  I sing
and for one not here no never no
never
            my heart
                  I fling.


Awake all night
My eyes drink up
each beam of moon
      its shining fill
      yet, at night,
and in these times,
      who deserves
to toss and turn
      alone.


But it is day!
      Companions, now come
      in raising praise
we'll raise the sun
      burn up in light
      and bathe
remembering how
when one has fled the earth

the senses I love more
still more each sense I
come to love
and more the sun
I want and wish.

It is an image of
                    oblivion.

You burn me up.
        Disrobing from heaven love
tears me limb from limb, rattles me
            miserable sweet,
        a crawling beast.
Wind beat me my tree my chest
you hate my very thought
you say 'against your will'.

Yet you the one appointed,
        chanted,  as you
                        chose
        to give me love
                            your neck

how many times
with flowers adorned
        anointed
there was
no dance
        to which we
        did not go.

The words I cannot weave
the love I cannot speak
ripened too high to pick too

                              high to
                              reach.

Raise up the roof and sing abroad—
for they are newly wed—
they join : I witness :
          but as for me,
          my mind is two
there is nothing I would not trade
          for you

*MAY YOU SLEEP ON THE BREAST OF YOUR FRIEND :* AFTER SAPPHO

# AFTER H.D.

For love so foolish discerning
      In colour desiring
Beyond reach
          Reaching
      Transposing
          To voice
      In yearning
The spirit of song
      Bittersweet

Not one colour alone
But all
      At once
Not one rose
But all flowers
      Unfolding

She, of
      no
island
      no
country
      no
continent
      no
imaginable
world of emotion
in our nets
      to be attained

But the end of an epoch, a
world entire, a coming glory,

a star, all colour, burning, unfolding,
> to destroy
> dead custom foundational,
> on which is hoisted
> what passes
> for life

> > Sung serpent tongue
> > ironical, aflame:

> > > To sing,
not even in abstract contemplation,
not for beauty but wisdom
who seemed to herself a body
dead among the living
> how to be kindled
> > bleeding
> > possibility
> > binding unbinding tight
the opening of the skies

A Name
> the sea itself
> the waves unravelling unleashing
> untrammelled nets from deep
> not what hinders or impedes
> but weaves unravels
breaking but not broken
tortured and torturing
making and taking up
> on vibrating air vibrating
> > string;

> On string vibrating

Voice syllables stringing
Singing
      of lover on lover
of colour on colour
      of flower on flower
as objects transforming
              —all colour
                  all roses
                          rising
            In colour all
colour           desiring
each fragment fragrant witness wafting
fragrant still
      O palimpsest
of love

# INTERLUDE

Hard hurts the heart
what was poured to its mould
and made in its name
How that heart was shaped
to receive the one semblance of a value
a living           melding
How continue
as of old

*

What underwrites,
in cases of loss or damage?
Who guarantees,
in times alone?

As that day so soon will fall
in which so soon we'll fail, asking
What promise in happiness
will ever so violently  be kept?

Yet Love, give so much love.

And trust, though what evidence in hand
as shame is cost tattooed
if cleaned, interned within
accepted for telling exchange.

Narrate for survival suffice, hold to
what ever would in safety prove.

*

may you sleep on the breast of your friend

## KYPRIS POEM

How can one not hurt
whom one loves and wishes to re-
call? Simple, Stop longing
                    for that...
the unknown sex of the beloved
            desire...releasing...

Instead fit right object to right affect
for right cause taming and subduing
put a check to extending limits
in
            the
                        cut
                                    space
                                                out
fill it in with right and matching love
to be a muse or bride.

But
who
are you
how often
you do come
to mind

And call
            on call
in transmission is scrambled
to the weakest signal spark
the weakest beating heart.

How often? Check. O placating

parent,
           why
that you told me
                        vainly to split
with severed vein in binding wound all sutured up
never ceasing to be a bleeding line, a tie.

Why say to me
                        sever
a natural line or grain
As a cleaver cuts meat
his love is pain
(though he calls it most
bounteous gift)

Releasing desire ...
relinquished...
pierced and young

# FRAGMENT

ugly Muse
who won't never
leave

with bile in throat
stuck to flow
and scorch

Melter of limbs
ruinous god

in changes
my solo
run down

# EPILOGUE: SONG

Rain out of
season in sun
delayed, burst
on burnt earth,
birthed out of shade,
intricate then dropped
blossom in opening cascade

# THE PROBLEM, THE QUESTIONS,
# THE POEM (PART II)

## ( F O U R )

## THE QUESTIONS

The person opposite screams and sighs the day's frustrations
      in everyone's lives,
saying who are we all are we all which we who know this,
      try it on for size.


Why does the sun always go in?


With a good ear can you hear the world, what does it say?


Leaning in and learning, open to everything.


There is hope in the eyes open wide to the size and the sound
of the secret things that explode in the night but on high, things
look very different. Someone. I think I'm low down, the view
from the ground.
This is the side I want, the side I'm on.


Watching eating made sick and together in mess and every
thing that leaks did it happen that anyone might try to know
the difference between *being in love* and *loving*, prolonged in
tender care beyond a practiced property hold, prolonged,
however
to do it, how long.



What to do,
where there was so too much wind,
& all the sea is dying.

# THE PROBLEM

The poem, the person, needing a new theory of the subject, but generally careless or useless or whichever one of those was not prolonged thought enough, not knowing what's said in a rhythmic knowledge paradigm instinctive, answering to a higher knowledge someone screamed and we all believe it, half-believed, to be true, almost in tears.

Everything.

# THE POEM

As poison breathed in. As eaten flowers.

As easy as the weather. Crossing the wide sea.

With garlands and wreaths crowning, bringing back the idea of the festival, those who speak, giving voice to the seasons and the universal laments of love's idealized individualized mythical holding frame. This is how things go on.


Bridging the narrow sea.


The ship. The vessel.

The craft. The rock.

The mud.

It runs. Wet or dry. What runs out. Things get started. Get stuck.

The string hits me in the gut. Things begin below.

Inside Ravel's tiny face, coming out of Rachmaninov's huge heart, the reiterated melody underneath under arpeggiated decorated leading strain in the winds makes my heart to sing. Or was and is it to *collapse: turn it off*, NO, NO, IT WAS *TOO MUCH*! I prefer order. Some idea. It was as a chorus of nymphs. Scherzo or schizoid.

It was as a chorus who had not been and were not lead, threatening to break out of the heart's bounds set up, of decency, its control, its propriety. This was what it *could* have been. Or: it was the disguised proprietorial force of the permission given and tacitly imposed, to act and lounge, cavort, in the way right pleasing to the leading male eye.

With castanets.

Bells and tambourines.

Strings, fiddles, bows, giant resounding, gold resounding, giant gold rings.

Water flies up off the land, goes back round again. It all falls off the back. You fall off the globe. We all fall down.

There is all in all always very much too little, all too so much.

After everything.

To go down.

This is a pastoral. This is the entire experience of land. Have you tried the order of a fine style, a social ordering in nature, everyone's gardens, remedial, with the cleanest idea of order. I love to break up and fail.

But this is so bright. So dark. Senses get confused—confusing! —an immense world of delight—open—closed—after coming down the sun beats down its tune. Making the sky ring.

Sing:

Dionysus going to the sun, Apollo going to the moon.

Seasons are ripe for walking in endurance.

It starts dark. It goes dark. It gets up. It burns too much, too light, too bright, the shadow which is not a shadow but the most brilliant light figured divine and blinding, against death. As death. It is a life that binds back to a synthetic bleeding wound.

You throw away life in the river. Some people do this. They do or do not want to see you do this. How much you value this thing, this moment. It is as the sun getting up, the dissonance makes it stark triumphant, Ravel with one arm, the poet with one claw, the spread clasping chime that would hold everything in, his arms by his side. Waving a hand, the greatness of his specific gesture. It would make the world cohere in silly dropping off.

A landscape is big, and wide.

Where everything starts obscured in the wood the guide takes your hand, the route takes you aside. It takes your side, it is the road travelled by a few laughing at the grass mown, or not mown, in the sun. Heads bob in the lake, frozen still, you kick a few, witness participant in mute suffering. Tell me

your name. It loves to be told, to be talked to. Where looking at the sun solves the feeling, looking up at the sky. Out of the machine the box drops down. It is a borne grace solving everything.


It was wrong, the wrong movement. The birds dipping up to the sky. Felt lost in spite of it all, a bird swooped to touch the head, with blood on its beak. There was some limb you had lost. Travelling.

International shipping is free.

Things diverse get stitched together, made to cohere. Rhapsody.

From nervous uncertainty to making it a reality. To be the master of your own career. Work blues winning gold. I strained to exert right muscle form, to see.

With art comes science, comes social responsibility. The feeling is as of a march. Face stuffed. Face full. Dip and swerve.

Follow the curve. Where does the river go. The bodies come back home. Going underground, be my guide. It all flows so bad, hurts so much to tell. It is natural, conscious, at a steady state of claimed transcendent experience in groups, regulating air going in, coming out; it is as easy to breathe, as to not breathe, all solved with the right time to pay easily enough attention to the specific focussed group bodies concentrated upon, with the right time for exercise and for the right of frame of mind. Poetry is like this. I can't sit still.

In no experience of freedom, recurring it will bite, what is that sound. Already seen. Will someone please unlock the key. The door swings wide. It is my head you see inside, it is the whole solution washing everything clean. We will work through things and we will dream.

Things getting harder, much suddenly catastrophe flowed over the banks. Money was real, or not real, the figures were hard to tell from the figurations, the figurations from the figurines, the toys let loose, the controlling paper heart.

Economy flows.

Economies of flow, flow.

Wasted down the drain.

After a while it gets hard to get up again, stuck forever you get used to lying, to lying there, on your back suddenly the top seems wider than anything down here below, going *above* all the clouds, perched in the wisps and the blue.

Whispers of heavenly breath.

Intimations of some obscure and exciting morality.

The mountain range is big. The eye can describe, so many things, the head moving, from side to side. But there is just as much in the face I do not have. How much anyone could read.

In fragments. Like speech.

Of speech. The stomach knots.

Waiting in the wings, flying, performing, collapsing, falling off the stage.

## THE QUESTIONS

To be making
what make, of self.

Which thing.

Who knew.

This poem is made from blood.

This pen is made from blood. This hand.

You, me, we who are what want
the poem wants.

Want what,
what proposition.

What question.

You and others around you.

## THE POEM

It all turns, returns.

The land falls, is worked on, worked upon, changed, the scene of shame not changing though transformed, when we work through our secrets what privacies, what privations, coming in, coming up.

Moving forward in line, turning, overturning.

Against what measure. Hold.

One thing sets off another thing, we do not reach the end or the margin.

But how to change the things that kill to the things that live, the things that kill the things that live, alternating or altering in sync and breaking as work the hold of work, the holding on, the holding down, the merely holding up.

Earth is a material thing which we are living in.

You are.

Materially, you are poor.

Leaves keep falling from the trees.


Things change. You are changed.


The wind, and pain, we will never be taken, will we never be taken, will we paint the day to be right up there on view, the highest point, our loss?

Don't you ever want to come back?

It is OK, and no one dies.


All I amount to, this is all I will amount to, becoming the flowers, parading the garden round, telling the lilting time.

They were transformed to a scented and fixed safety-in-mourning, decoration forever forgetting and reminding of its origin.

The sweetest thing.

## THE PROBLEM

Staying out in the cold until so cold you cannot move, cannot move on; night and day ordering everything.

Compulsory homosociality, the great chain of being.

How to deal with things. These acts. No. How to stop them. Make them stop.

Stop. In abdication to remove each layer. Was law an ethics, ethics here a law, where in violence it stopped, making *what* law, saying vengeance or prevention as *what* law; or to consider it rather, as merely or more importantly the necessary reflex, the strategy, of survival itself. Being really, how to live, what this might mean you might be made to have to do. The you is split. Around the defence or denial of the bad act, the boys band together. Together they get a new tattoo.

Before abolition, the necessity of conflict.

The flame, almost to my face.

Drowning out song with my teeth.

The flame rose so high, and went out again.

Things coming in so close. Things burning, and touching. Flinching, and wounding. Things clenching, tightening, and binding.

Blinding. The body broken, or broken into. Close in. Closed down.

Automatic reaction broke out.

It was hard to see how to get out.

Where to start.

To know it not alive. Enclosed the fore-closed, the un-remembered act. It kept coming back in everything.

But work it through. Never stop thinking. This is how to begin. By its completion the new basis, in sequence in passion arriving, the start of a new venturing.

## ( F I V E )

## THE PROBLEM

What it means to start and end, wherever raised—who raised—
the voices of the dead, what voices of what dead, what specific
dead, what dead trash left cheap out of history and language,
the history of language, scoured off, wiped clean as a filthy rag
in history's bin. The shit seeping into the citadel, the memorial,
to those who were, to that which was, but was not seen; to
those choked in speech, their stammering.

The voice, in dream: *What will we do with all these dead?*

Dead to law, dead in law, dead to bring to life, to make living,
the living, speaking ordering of the living, speaking, ordered
thing, even that thing so low down as the poor basic subject
selling what laboured thing in bodily capacity they have, thus
to exchange, to have their being.

To memorialize, building something other than mausoleums,
in memories of solidarity, in memory's solidarity, its possibility,
building.

In order to bring to life that which never was allowed to live.

To destroy the palace itself, built on bones, built screaming, from
a formed and forming silencing, on the choking of the names.

In order to build what has not been.

What thing in the future lit up, projected back as shadow in
the poem. Waste speaks back. The mouth clogs up. You lap

it up, expel it out, you try to make that thing to exist outside.

In the sun the sea dries up. To be in so far, so far in, so far below, in water without light.

It has not ever been fulfilled.

What love was, was really believed. Was it ever really believed, was it retrieved, where it located itself in the dispensation raised whatever head would do for fixity? Things keep getting made into things, these things, into other things.

Some of these things are people.

What can you do?

It was hard to see how it all got out.

It was so close in.

## THE QUESTIONS

And the question remains.

Don't you ever?

Want, what, want. Being in wanting. Inclining and turning away.

Having been made so blind.

Being made so blind.

Made so blind.

Only every day.

# THE POEM

You can die without ever having seen anything. The objects arranged before were endlessly spread and endlessly pleasing in their ordering, and their re-ordering. It was thought at the time that things could never have been more beautiful, were as beautiful, as they have ever been. And this was as true in possibility as it was false in actuality, the dream of it threatening to unfold its beautifully self-sufficient idea of the order of things, sufficient and perfected, within its limits. To already have that thing, that idea, as an object, made out of that collection or collation of objects; or a feeling, harder to define, roused to be turned in that particular direction; to be moved, as the idea of satisfaction must exist in negotiation this completion widely troubling, never known until lost, its retrospective ordering as the idea of happiness spreads in whatever configuration to be unspoken in felt sharing.

The idea of things that have not been known.

The things I love the most in the music are where its beauty absolutely *is in no way* perfected, perfected only in the clearest knowing of all that could slip from the fullness up-swelling, where no one can live.

Some tried. Across the land the flowers are out, have been cut, harvested, cleared aside. The idea of wildness. This is doing this, and this is this thing; the assertion in statement is wish, proclaims magic, thinks the words could really be the work that acts on things in the world, as a thing transforming.

But also useless value.

So the climax cuts back, is dodged, is false, built up to and down from. The conclusions are always what are most untrue, in resolution a known place-holder for how the thing ends; but this is never, afterwards, what's come back to.

So the holding back, the holding in, the pleasing knowledge of the inadequacy of the idea of fulfilled comfort, even in the biggest heart, gives expression. But even that is evasive, and it is the turning aside, to want to be so easily touched, so easily hurt, that is the cultivated sensitivity sensation burns off, and things are sharp and knowing.

And this sharp knowledge is what must be had, must slice away the blind, be sure, saying no, that there are some for whom the gentle affirmation of light only makes the sight of a grimy dark the worse to bear, never even being allowed to have the life whose space as leisure would unfold beyond a faint felt numbing spoken loud, as the screech unending after the explosion reduced to heart-beat in every second second pumping, going, straining, restraining.

Does it get so dirty. How it gets to be so dirty. How it is.

Does it get hard to do all things, then, existing only in the condition of moving meat.

Eat up.

Whatever it means to rest. To pause. Cut flowers. But it is not said. It is decay. Come back. Come back and live.

It hurts to work to sing, taking work to justify any condition of being thus, in work, or out of it – or love, things provided of, or for. You can share this with the world.

To say that love is this, that life is, this colour, this shade, this set of actions or non-actions, this ethics, this ordered or dis-ordered law or not-law, this arrangement of dispensations towards the world that is this size, could be made up or shrunk down. That this is, the condition or the size, *is* this small or this impossibly wide, a task so big un-ending.

## THE QUESTIONS

Hot ash in the eye. *It isn't even warm.*

Air knows no borders.

Does it get hard to breathe?

Nothing you've done or ever will do is good enough.

What is the relation between grammar and love?

What is the distance in the voice through the speaking implement spanning across, and shrinking in?

Things "come to me", but do I go, to them? To go away, absent, abdicate. What presence predicates the things that seem offered as gift, existence justified as this pleasing attentive capturing, manifested as beneficent love, to be so in love, with the things and the people of this world, with the children and the kites and the diverse local colour, and the bright colours, and the multifarious possibilities you can ask them questions, imagining their lives, not really ever hoping for that curiosity to be returned, not cared in play they swim up to you, or merely near you, not even to you, and go away, how far such attentive excitement is really relation in unfolding. So easy it's not even true.

The thing, coming to me, to my attention. The things. Are there, for your delight.

I made a thing of pleasure, a lovely thing. Was thus delighted, delighting.

This went so far before it broke. Where things run out.

The song in the throat, at the back of the mouth.

The song, blinding.

In it or out of it, the thing.

Or come to it *this* way. The wheels almost ran you over. You will almost always be over there. You will almost always be run over by the wheels. The cogs.

But speak from there.

Get up.

To be let in.

Take it.

What hope raised.

Take hold.

Get out.

Go on.

## ( S I X )

# THE POEM

Who do not magnetize bullets.

To say that now direction will always be predicated, the compass spun, in the directions which delineate economic ordering: within the bounded ring, arrived at with whose consent—*nomos; eikos*, the direction and the space marked out in metaphor as home. But *we* also live here, live within. Delimit. Stop.

In reconfiguring. To have to accept defeat without dying to action.

Inside, what outside can be constituted? Where? In what places?

Analogous. I do not want to turn to the arcane, except if it is real. When it is real, in figuring. Metaphor. Our mouths. From inside—which—what; this—from which outside.

It works.

The terms, as moral injunction. Instruments of currency. It demands austerity.

Who is it speaks, speaks back, speaks to. What things bring happiness. How, by whom defined. The web spun from the tree to the table to the pin, attached itself to my face, unseen until lit up in the sun. The scene as a whole was calm. The distance that can not, literally, be imagined. Touch turns golden. Fields seep golden, black. Oil anointing their heads. There is a crown, and it is lifted, deposited, to the head it fits, melding to their shape, or they to its, golden.

The wonder is, the clean and desperate; the desperately clean. Does it get dirty. Not that to which one is called, but the condition in which that calling takes place, the already-established names. Go against. To know them, and to go against them, is the reverse of alchemy, or takes as source that shit as talking waste talks back. It convulses, it writhes, in fits and bursting starts it brings itself to speech, in places forming space where an allowance might be forced and formed, for the permission, the capacity to speak. To be called, to recall, in bands, allowing no freezing gold in place of light from which, as yet, we cannot eat and grow.

It is blinding dark.

In the sea, below it. Fish, instinctive, breathe water. Flop. Flesh, its instinctive flinch knows deeply negative, felt in this the allowing, to be or not to be, human. Flesh rebels. Flesh controlled, the social, reaction, imagined flesh, its origin there, instinct, imposition, of control, not seeking consent, passed off as need.

*An unqualified good*. Hierarchy negotiates its way in law, but is law too that which must be appealed to as stock of ethics, however degraded, filtrated, silted mud and sand in the wet congealing of abused rule. The rule of abuse. Rule, to control violence, or the violence, of control, where else to come from. To depart. In the end the prime ethics, or the ethic that is most present and therefore, at this moment, first, is the question of survival. How to organize it. Beat. This which makes what law.

It stretches to my screen. It stretches my skin. It screeches, your skin, will not be heard, will not be seen. The marks stretch wide and deep. Incessantly bleeds, leaks, gets packaged, gets packed up. Wheels. Turns. Converts. Gets turned to lump. It is sad in your throat. Expel a lump. It is shit to speak. Who gets spoken to, shouted over, in place. Gone to waste. Gone to ground. *As* waste, *as* ground. The speaking ground spoken from.

## THE PROBLEM

Today I wrote in the company of men. The pages were fully and duly filled.

The duty, fulfilled. To uphold.

As category, as object, repeat, disrupt. Tread out the line. In stigma they tell the women what to do.

Then, to have done with the judgement of men! So falling in politics. Affection spreads. The boyfriend blown up to fill the sky, the stretching escaped void filled with fundamentally altered relations to others, new modes of social being. The tilt was forced, it must be corrected. After a time, you might be allowed back in.

Only in apartness being able to remove the internalized mechanism transmuted and transmitted, of a competitive striving for the prime-cut trophy role. In the token place. It gets passed around. The ranks open up to close in.

But this apartness is together a resolve.

Separate. Disassociate. The bonds pull back. Given up, in the name of love. I want the ethics to be better, not to teach but to learn, to listen. Your back is to the door. A hole in the door gets shut in. The voices outside get shut out. You shout out, denounce. These bands band together, the tacit agreement, the bonds of the group already lived in, slept in, spoken in, letting in, the mode of living already assented to, assenting. The quarrel in print. The qualification, the only peace maker.

*If.*
    What.
*But.*
    Not.
*Is.*

Step back. Shut up. Debate opens up, or it shuts down. The flowers here are noxious, they cover up the smell of shit. The rhetoric is right, and in life it seems never to be applied. Get started. Get stuck. Try again. All our hopes down the drain. Whoever we are to say. Whoever I am to breathe authority.

This, is what. What righteousness offered up. Spat up breath.

How you can even speak to these people.

## THE QUESTIONS

And who speaks with those dead to law?

Giving up bits of the body to sell. Some of them leak, give out, emit.

Fluidly mobile, malleable in shape. Squeezing in at the door, in at the gate. The crack. Into the crate.

Great. These are gifts given without consent. In work, in loving look. Imaging what it would be, to see without the eyes of a commodity. Wanting not to want, said to be wanting, to lack.

Blind. Drawn to what we love. By what objects shaped, shaping? By what objects you break.

The waves, they break. The day, it will break. Night is so short an escape, it will break. The heart. The snapping bone. Flesh rubs off the fingers, skinned, to the bone. As this malleable solid lump. Fungible as fuck. Mutable and sad.

Death is on its way. Death as day. Death on the shoulders of a living assertion on objects, on land, made to be cast in a pillar of chipped-off stone or salt, looking back. Looted, to make the city. To build. Foundational. This is basic shit.

The punishment in fire was not because they shared their love across the rigid property-dispensation of the gender relation, growing hard the wrong way, but because they asked to offer up the visitors of guests for abuse. Received not the strangers. This is why their city burned in flames.

So her look back was not in memory of some supposed sexual immorality, but a longing for the hospitality that had not been had, the model, of two ethical bodies, protecting the guest, not giving them up. That look in memory, of what might have been, from the condition of exodus, of flight. This pillar is, then, the freezing of that yearning, that memory. But the city burned in flames. And it all went wrong from there. The father, knowing his daughters, in desperation prolonging his line. The absolute of ownership.

Law as crime.

## THE POEM

The dance has turned to death; and yet here I am still studying or gently revelling in the waltz, so gently moved by its restrained-exuberant capacity, so profoundly moved by its capacious-melancholic unravelling. Still stuck inside the small face, still stuck inside the big heart.

The door to the world come off on its hinges. The framing worldly order itself! What comes through, that which was hidden, revealed. That Law defining itself against Law as such, as it has been. Now. It must be the *victim* defines the law. Not Nature instates, but nonetheless in material, in practical truth, what to do. Outside that condition, in victimhood, what over-turns, is re-newed, from below:

Will it so.

The end. I do not want this world as it is. But teach me to know this, holding on.

The dream of violence must be to end violence. This is the aim, as politics. Aesthetics has consistently failed to live up to this, in its piteous regard, the wilting flower celebrates its trampled condition of mud, or the imagined bounteous flow of blood from the erased heads of state, cartoonish in their bleeding. A poverty of imagination, the special pleasure of our time, no admittance save on vacation. When violence becomes terror, what line to draw. The work must work harder; must be more difficult, in writing, in speech, to imagine what we mean when we say these things are the things we believe in.

To think about this question of law.

To chaos again. To law. Flip it around. To figure it as no retainer fixed, but the remnant siphoned off that in waste forms against the chaos of bourgeois Law as that petrified relation of rule, that apparatus in class interest fixed and fixing. That remnant, then, its own *katechon*, restraint on such chaos; restraint figured by the powers as chaos itself.

Says the man stammering before the magistrate, I will burn down your courts. Says the woman in social silencing, in social dying, I will burn down your gender, its closing-down, its networks of law. Against them, As instruments of law, not only the manifest agents, their uniformed body suits, but those agents enacting in daily practice the active harm acts on humans as propertied object, the freest love. That x that turns person, to thing; that *x* they are made to desire as 'love'. In harmony played, this tune, even outside the public sphere, the shattering confines of its lie, enforced, even outside the manifest agents, in force, in posited extreme the old norms rear their head as plain as day and just as deathly hid.

I want to know you are reading this. Tell me it's wrong, if it's wrong. Tell me, shut up in, or in glimpsed instance, in resistance organizing, continuing, breaking out against, this time.

Starving for food, for love, stopping just at the edge of the sea.

## THE PROBLEM, THE QUESTIONS, THE POEM

But the movement is inexpressibly long, and so social in private it is not known. Yet believing its testing, its trying, in private prefiguring. The movement, then, is long. Or, as far as the breaking dawn of such distinction in loving glimpse and fear might seem. The thing, can it even be said to exist? As a host of moist feelings, inclinings, the shining drop of water lifted off the surface of the sea. Things are flowing, and they are changing. The worst is to see the faces trodden down, trodden in. Walking past the start lost for all time.

Stop. You begin. The conditions. The problems. The song shook out in singing. The changes wrung on.

As simple promise. The change. One thing for another thing.

As changing. The language read in to a world of things. Change them.

It is a fantasy and there are hundreds of them.

The moist utopia. The tamed. The wild.

An instrument of delicacy becomes the most aggressive thing.

# LOVE IS A DANGEROUS NECESSITY

\*

HUMANS, we're all here, but I think we can do better,
though we're all tired, and exhausted, and afraid.
Life will be everything, or it will be nothing;
The firmament is so vast it is unbelievable,
it contains everything we might try to be,
and all we cannot be—

But O my face and O my heart,
how can we POSSIBLY *live* when others are dying?

\*

They have kidnapped our poets, pledged our hearts to monsters,
at the front lines of the aristocracy of labour, in the halls of the
      rich;
Bourgeois reactionaries make everything unclean, face it,
And it is those with most sophistication who are most simply
      cruel,
They say that Everything we believe or believe in is a crime.
Mass movements fail and fall into the shards of glass refracting the
rainbow of hope doubly in covenant reneging on promise,
a reconciliation between earth and sky, the answer to each
      anguished cry,
that basic image of hunger the point at which any analysis
      must begin.

\*

Poet be a worker, the leader said; knowing what work
you will have to do, what will you choose?
Happiness is the demand that no one on earth will
ever be born into any of this filth and fuckery again—
and yet, each half step more unbearable than the last,
we get sick and hungry all the time.

\*

Is being alive worse than death, in a world
where there are worse things than to die?

What have we become?

As any lullaby draws breath tenderly against death,
What will we *do* in life, listening to the
insane litanies of the dead not counted for;
What will we *do*, breaking up language into
little numbered bits invented by the patriarchy?

*

The world turns. The wall falls down.
The ground falls down. The earth opens up.

Language is not private property,
rhyme is everyone's un-
alienated dead labour, it rises and falls,
collapses in parody,
the present in the guise of the past,
the future's horizon ever-diminishing—
but through it nonetheless
We will remember the dead and do everything we can
to help them win.

*

I sing the body pathetic, the body dirempted;
the body collective, the body corrected;
The function of my words is to memorialize the
speech of my comrades and friends, and
None of this is provisional:
I will try out every position and come to believe the rhetoric
I inhabit, not knowing the truth of any of this until I do it, for
NO ONE is EVER really alone, and Love is a dangerous
          necessity—
the hope that everything might turn out well, the crepuscular
glow of all that hope, its shining immensity
witnessed barely but witnessed yet—


Later we will check all these things up in the
dictionary of accumulated human wisdom and history,
knowing the class basis of everything and the right way to
          morally be,
how to reconcile ourselves to the transience of life,
from organism as orgasm to bodily decay;
but for now, be as abject or the best you can possibly ever be,
knowing that your poem knows or could know more than you
and might yet be infinitely free—
and, in spite of EVERYTHING, join me.

# RELIEF EFFORTS

# TERMS AND CONDITIONS

Can you use this?

Can anyone use this?
Why not?

fire waned sun

open window

In
conditioned catastrophe
boxed items, shared
spilled spoils,
human backs,
the secret jokes of the stars'
winking constellation weeping, looking down


Without the arbitrary bonds of love
no provision or
protection
affords,
the shell against denial

Darts of friendship or love like shots in the dark.

The light
        urge
                rising
and the gravity that pushes back down,
the constant motion, the sky
shut off

or the fantasy of it,
burning bright and blind and brilliant
in some other world yearned for,
swooping then
      falling and crawling
to conditions of learned violence,
structures of learned dominance—
in object expense invested,
in falling and catching
rituals of display

Doing justice in epic, the behaviour of the whole
representational scheme
life internalised acted / outer shell—
at edges shoved back,
framed small

Tell me the truth about never having enough.
Teach me the truth about being always so satisfied.
Tell me the best, most broken secret places
To be hidden in and to hide.

How to live through the damage given the name of desire, to and
in its name; histories as form and still they shape, that Obstacle
dodged comes back: whatever it is, that cannot be processed,
works away, corrodes within; in operation the incisions multiple
and so precise, precise and all too numinous to be felt.

Bury the dead in the water,
bury them in the sea,
burn up the corpse in the park. Remains.

That no event, single, would overthrow or erase the violence
of what's named progress in time—progression in body fabric
facet, social sutured wound to feed—ed and cast aside, to cell
or heap;

Elegantly shuttered up,
too late and closed;
incapable of speech.

More now than ever before, if it were to split open, it would
immediately reconstitute itself, bigger than ever, and twice as
smooth.

From each pyre, from each wreath draped sombre song: most
pathetic wavering trill. In power distributed, stretched so thin,
you think of what object as collective wish you made, and the
individual hopes twisted within that organising web.

However this could not happen, however much though in mourning still refrain returns; Ceaselessly. A children's game about death, and the formation of the group; training for loss; easy replacement object switch;

So Trill endlessly alone.

To the dog a bone, a gesture of impossibility: cataloguing each abuse, each measurement, each mode, weighed in hand and heart and brain, to drop it all in visible throwing up of hands abysmally, beyond reach.

In veils of transparency having proved always to have been in disguises clothed, in clothes disguised, in songs that promise much said ceremony bedraggled wreath for wraith.

So saying this ending of what is named as world, the abolition of all things: what vision of history, No one, no goal, singular and full too easily dreamed to be fulfilled.

Yet in defence not to be resigned.
Somewhere you have to start. Somehow.

# A SONG FOR LEAVING
*After Rilke*

Can it be possible that I never saw you
before you left, what imprint of your face
remains in mind and what of you in heavy heart to say
but that until the end of time you destroyed: that
this will be the memory of you.

That you felt the need to possess
     self and
everything
beyond possession
as now in accumulating
         it is trapped;
what could not be spelled out,
could not be read nor
lived, save where the dead, none for
     such possessiveness
     shed an ounce of care,
being nothing and accumulated the memory
shared, projected back.

Where else but away to live,
that place which is no place,
where
     in sleep
the dead
walk unsafely
not to be buried,
walk unsound
not in rest laid
out, no hopes fulfilled?

On you we work out our despair.

Brushed each to the other in
shared extinction with
customary peaceful respect in a
glance, this fantasy we have, and you,
                    do not feel
you stand out, stand alone,
on the fringes of the group
with the burden of all grief not borne
by you alone, though so it seemed;

Those enormous terms not for us, no victory
but endurance all we have
past loss in death and like that living loss
in all of us felt, closed off;
betrayal daily of what we know
or glimpse in straining instant catching glint
To say you would have lasted or lived for this is a petty
appearance, some re-constructing dream
as unheard music, sweet deferral forced;
not for that would expect you to wait, this no
comparative reproach,

when to survive it at
                    all
is unbearably
        a triumph of the heart
barely and at
        what
                    cost
                        borne,

beyond love and in its name.

## LETTERS TO

Writing about the heart in the houses of the rich
trees that grow inside, break out painful,
doleful what the hand receives, then hurt retreats,
what ground is gained, where you stand,
rising not for the sake of ascent in itself,
and descent of death as the other side
of what action is figured as necessary to take.

You have a feeling contradicts. You struggle.
In the stammer and in the pause, the strength,
wherein weakness maintains no glimpse at the end,
holds out, we take care of our own. Who we are,
who the angel who is

                    not us

                         said,

              where the figuring
of flying as singing and the rise and fall
fell too hard, bruised the head in the hole in the earth.

Here the sentences run short. Here the well is dry in a
drenching time. You attune to the tide, away from
affairs, pace the corridors with the mountains and
flight, write something down at least, it gets done, over
winter, over melting forming, the sounds ringing
for one who has never seen light, who has never
but in dreams been cleaned by palpable bright
shining visiting.

In letters will he advise, tell you
this is what it's like.

                    Having objects in your life.
Things that sustain you. Re-arrange, what violent

alarm for the parents of the poet, the furniture,
the feelings. Spending hours in a castle unruined,
forming thoughts not theories how to conduct
one's life. You must change, shift, what harm
gets done, better learning fast, better not learning
what grinds out in the daily
getting of things, arranging,
                    the maintained
sense of a self not broken too totally
apart, not made as a patch-work walking corpse
from others' imaginings, finding the fractious
sustaining sociality of the others in the carriage,
the comrades, not alone on the
kitchen table pressed bleak.

What traces remain.
No painless escape.

What this other thing is,
the others there, where we do go
from here, what it is
still to learn, hold in trust
the line that comes last but not finally
the ending not working
for its mending, for its making,
                    continuing
for its taking shape,
driving away, being driven,
learning to
        promise provisional
yet promise in truth.

# RELIEF EFFORTS
## *IN WINTER, FOR LIGHT*

### 1.

Singing, in winter, of the need to
go past goodbyes as if they were already,
like seasons passing, gone:
for going read embracing, dying,
condition of perpetual departing, re-making,
shattering as a ringing glass on seeing, hearing
report, knowing that nothing, oscillating from
its centre in order, ordering debris scattered, shattered
in the realm of remains
parts without number on the numbered pile in counting
unsayable saying, to this adding and cancelling the sum

for under winter is a winter so lasting
that, hibernating, your heart resists, withstands
any way it can

storm without name
fade away
it can be said but is it cruel to kindle
a shack a shelter
from desire trembling
building
in air or sky

I can't see the poem but I can hear it breathing
who let it in

## 2.

In winter's going
some poet was saying
you must come back singing
what's buried deeper
the frost without thaw

What's buried deep
the flaw a
      flake a
spark
detached piece
      blown
burst out
      in dark
      : burst or squall
rent
      : rift
broke off
      in drift

      Then take this part
Broke to a fragment singing
parts, the whole, not wholly complete
not wholly to repeat
      though desiring repeating re-
plenishing
stock in
      this
      time
      of
defeat.

In this time...
Last straw
drawn
warming rest

Slow comes the dawn
drawn faces when it comes
facing the day we had not slept,
stayed in

Stocking up
supply, providing for
offered guest, kept
at arm's length
to measure out
the test.

This is how I set out:
I set my store by this
though chewed and swept by drift
give my word
       heard faint

winter-
       swept,
wind-set,

Leaving the house
following
The literal ways of the heart,
          the vessels, passages,
          set to a tongue in-
          toning
the conflicts of emotion and direction,

all the way
the image, beyond reasonable doubt,
the concentrate.

Warm within
          and hiding.
Scant relief
          abiding.

I watched it, ears still ringing,
dreaming of completeness
no adequate
          eloquence
                    provides,

yet seeking
respite, to stitch together
what would be bearable in this world,
tokens given, the parts that fall into your lap,
                    in
                              the
          fragments that catch
a warming tune, which, warning,
burns yet bright if waning
to sustain us through the way.

No digest it turns continuing,
It churns against the gut
in sweet ascent of sad lament,
well anyway all we had, the mouth
dried out, hung up. Though I borrow steel
my flesh be cold, my flesh be weak be softer than the
toughness peeled:—

So take me to the end, the place
beyond all reasonable hope.
Down where none are dying,
Where none need assert
In dumb harm.

Down where none are pushed aside,
where none asunder are swept to a
cracked neck a whole lost head:
what notes there streaming:

Clipped wing
      Broken thing
Little whole
      Tiny thing—

don't be ashamed of the tender dead
who tenderly may you clasp to your breast,
who last for a longer enduring
while. Do not succumb.

Of the proportion of relief to despair
heart thumping quiet in heat in
thickest thicket trim sometimes covered best.

Covered to attest in softness there
softest softness born of a hardness saddest
ringing in stung flinched hurt to be touched.
Felt to be flawed all the open cut exposed
hard and fast in the hidey hole I made
passed by the sign of a letter with key intact
and swallowed whole.

Have you been there?

Was it worth it?

Saying that you saw
        and sung
in going,
        passing,
A flame lit
to that melting
        thing
in losing it
only then to know
its dis-
appearing shape.

It fits and is mine.
Though it breaks
breaks up, is not,
no one's
one possession,
no cupped
                singular
                        coin
        minted with a
face obscure.

Not money, some other worth.
Not a thing made, endured,
preserved, posterity's claim,
impermanent swept.

Yet hear me out.

The poet with no head
says

That,
under winter, is another, endless winter:
Leap over that, with your heart.

Whatever is there interred, the turning back,
turning off stage, rock in drift of snow,
kingdom of glowing
glass,
ice on which clanging
sound, shining
sun—

your song—
melting—
and a way in the night-sense beginning,
though groaning under weight of snow and swinging
low, would over-power
power, death, disease:

breaking sweat, voraciously a
swelling, though fallen,
not saying the sun,
you have jubilation in your leaping over
in the death of that debt.

## 3.

Well in winter going down
Reckoning up
Change for a tune
A machine would play

Or just sounds exchanged
What beckons up the day

It's all we have saw frost saw
a blank.

They, of the wider standard,
of the higher
booked a place at the feast
it will rest
I guess enough for them
for us, less

It's the season
rejoice

if you don't have it
and if you don't
throw it away

you can't surrender what you don't have
but you can spit on that meagre possession nonetheless
                              spin with
caution cut to the cloth of
wind-whipped
running,
or steady walking, sharing,

with a caption spilling wild from the mouth,
a different song,
later to be figured a number of ways,
when at night you lie and talk
later write it down.

Oh big world!
Some things integral to the whole,
not known their concentrate,
as ramifications feeling our way in
to what it would feel to feel that,
and we know.

If we took away that letter we'd have what,
a quality of feeling only,
or all that the engagement meant, committing

holding to
That feeling
some call the sharp abutting end of brittle surviving.

Breath comes out, solidifies

This is old, a sign from the universe
we don't know, no longer trust
in. I mean after the end

something has to start again
you overheard.

And overhead where we crane our necks
to the brighter orbs
guiding lighter our thoughts
than in a city where clouds judge

head down
Will I make this my contract
with whoever will agree to listen.

Who loves secrecy
and who holds close
when what's kindest is to leave it alone.
When what's kindest is to leave.

Don't listen through the walls
don't play. Real cinema directly
set up. In the end, you pay.
You really mean it all.

Perform, rehearse, deliver
as if it could be tied up to one
packaged whole, one neat gifted
offering. Then we offer each other
things. This way we

work it out, in trust.
Establish regard.

I look into
I look forward to
your eyes.

How to talk it
is harder than most
care to admit;

In the end, you pace,
for you know that
despite silence's demand

Yet you've been told
and what you might seek to hold
preserved
        enfold
in habit to rise
comes to light

No place so deep abide.

Blink and close your eyes
some relief at least
relieved of duty for a while.

And who said what that was?
Who, what you have to do,
with whom, where the choice
aligning negotiating
what constitutes
truth.

Who committed in on-
going placing
of one foot after the other
often falling often

better could or should have done or
spoken well, spoke worse,
did so often fail,

And yet it was in the effort that,
without the heavy weight
of judging, or always with that,
carried though nervous with the name,
love, at minimum needed

care at least,
a spring arising,
a step anew.

# NO THING BY ITSELF

No thing by itself
and no thing by itself
and no thing by itself
alone

If the trees touch the sky in a poem it holds up
if I say it holds

         (Day burning on me
       Sun burning in me;

And if the eye
is broken by sun
or sky surrounding,
out-strung, in
     momentary
         momentum
            formed;

If the sky is not a map
but malleable
values imposed,
     bits of the roof of the world
     where there is no roof
     a room with head burst through,
parsed or passed over,
problems of navigation
in flickering return;

If in slippage the compensations
of fictive omnipotence fail
in weakness revealed

Please ensure that you turn
Attend
to turn of breath returning

No thing by itself
facing
the face of the world

# THREE SONGS

SONG ONE

Then the earth arose
it spread unclosed
the joins were hid

Wrapped up and wrapt
in repeating change
the light faded and
speaking shades
                    amazed us
singing through our
mouths enclosing
projects for worlds not
yet fulfilled

So rapped out
and received re
turning knock:
an eyeful an ear
                    attuned,
full blanket folds it
dropped its gift

The world fell full
face at the sound
of the trumpet
obscured; blared out in full

Fresh falls the rot
a taste of metal in
mouth Fanfare for

announcement
degraded

With full lung power
last words
no longer supported
yet summoned
summed up


      SONG TWO

      Then the I
      Was in bits
      Out-sourced,
      Out-Strung;

      Stung and stunned
      with splinters that cut and form.

      Day's burn, the warm
      medicinal
                    glow
      a salve applied,
      turned to a fresh stinging

      Chafing in splints
      Breaking shape


SONG THREE

Mend or amend
Amen

At adequate stretch
A named completion

But Blink and you'll see
Mistake wood
for trees
Fresh faced effacing

To duet with different things
dust in the mouth
when it opens to sing

Dues paid
Laying foundations
subject to shaking
Building temporary stations
in quiet question, hushed oblation;

Asking
who is that turning to greet
a new abidance
        in subsistence
        subsiding
Who does the following
And who does the hiding

If the platform is short
What alights
With fresh demands adapting

And from what heights
Do cries arise
In structures collapsing

Who's here to catch
the catch in the voice
or throw
or bawl

who's hear to hold
or hear the fall

# THE TENOR & THE VEHICLE

The instrument of hope, the vehicle, is stalled.
And for miles the road, when to get off it, the fork.
Where next to stop, a pause in the central movement
before the
                    crashing of
                         manu-
          factured climax
forces to a false instance con-
centrating expectancy in every second
it would shatter and seek to sort and sift,
to force the shift for this
to realise in its inhabitation, temporary spell.


Magic makes the act equal the object equal
the wish imposed, the wish grown or desired within,
projections on the back wall crumbles as it is built,
brick by hollow brick. My own unblinking cinch,
to bind to the others they hope so, as hard or as
fast, how measured on the scale. There is a line a
central empty space
                         which is the way in the word,
the zone, the line from nowhere to nowhere most
exactly placed, a window open on the exterior inside.


What else could we want and never name,
time is short. What could serve as report:
the fit place, the methods, the act follows on,
how to get outside.

# SPEAKING TURN
*FOR TOM RAWORTH*

       found

Nowhere when
suddenly
stanch

       found

It
every
where
breaking


       And
it
breaking
now

falls to the
altered
how

in
in
human
luxury
decency
dependent

it
moves

grinds
empty

at speed

forgets
yet

a kind of
good no
less

falls to the
quick
seen
slice

faith
ful to the
flesh

fear
trod the
fear the
flesh
sears

that the times
are not in
stead right

a heart
beating

false tears
torn

the times their
missed
repeating

*

I'd
faster
go

ordered

further
paced out
flank

fuck
I am faith
less

to the flag I
swear no
allegiance

in the centre
in the margins
scrawled

watch word
pass
go

re
sist de
sist systems
slot in
place

spot
check
spot
running
empty
fuelled

exorcise
exercise

what is
eating
my spine


                    *


give over
get well

                yes
adjust
possessed

tune in
speaking
turn

swapped
dial
volunteered

froze
or singed

songs done
done now
in code

dot dot
stopped or trailed
off

on off on off
doubted di
thered docked
& jumped sent home
with mouth sealed / up

who's done a good job
support
when they come
if they come
when they come

\*

very definitely

articles
the comfort of nouns

defiantly
against
designation
final
station

the best form
not ever
not even
now
enough

it is em
bedded here

but not
bedded down not
settled
in

make me a
pallet
cut
through

end of the line
move

# IT IS GOING TO BREAK

It
is going to break
                    and
                    this
is a figure for something;

Everybody talks
this is a figure for the weather,
the poem beginning when the
sun shines through the
crack in the door and the clouds,
dispersing light, melting hail.

Common environment
the face of the earth
natural or artificial
more or less real:

You would become the barometer
failing in predictions
                    announcing
                    anticipating
getting it wrong.

The poem never getting going,
the poem
                    getting by,
seeking a reason for being;

Out of sorts it sorts
                    arranges
subscribe for more

casually explained

Riding the lift
between earth and sky
digging to raise up
                below

This is a figure for something
tricked in the city
lost in the country
knowing that you see the lightning
before you hear the thunder

Before that the day
grows heavy
knowing that
it is going to break

This is a figure for collective response
which is rare but possible
gifts of the kingdom centre
the car from round the corner
the chink of the key against the
                glass in the bag
the scrape of the key in the lock
the creaking floor when anxieties enter
dull thud of feet on streets,
in alleys, main roads,
entrances, exits
main attraction
                side-show

Closer or        further
from the centre

                    pushed out
how does it appear as an image
how does this figure figure
illustrious, exemplary,
sweltering
                    and close


and slowly boiling the
pressure as it mounts in the
slow un-
bearable flatness of this day's be-
coming similar to any other,
hardening
into routine


This is a figure I
chose, was it the figure I
wanted;
have a sad moment


            under his eye


and ask your   self
is it going to break


In the flat surface,
from the flat centre


            slot to slot in place


Word for word exchanged
in condition of surrender
in condition in-
adequately to render

buffering
in real life
in the real life centre
too long
didn't read

Hardening into style
frozen into form
the catch-all to trap all the
semblance of living

      past
           slow
                electric
                     gates

faster
healthier
cheaper
more fun

nothing
beyond this point
nothing

it is going to break

## JUNE POEM

In the orbit
of the ambit
I gambled
on hope

In the orbit
of the ambit
I gambled
and these things I saw:

Seasons, suns, mist,
titles, squares, orbs, blocks,
        fucking up
from on high,
refusing to come down
until the right prompt called the cue.


My angels, my angles,
trying to get correct perspective
        adjusted
from the narrow side.

It is true that
The day was bright and my mouth was burning.

Washed in flame.


The moth evaded the lamp my jaw was locked to.

Wandering far in too-close proximity,

                    periodically
going up and down the stairs,
          the fulcrum,
the pivot whose knit tight-
ness began to unravel.

Contained and folded in on
itself, continued to flap.
The rain hit the window.

Do you think it happy,
do you think it important, to judge.

And what if they have no names to tell you
no names to tell you of?

There is a thing to speak
but it crumbles and disperses
in the wrong register
in the fractured attempts
at responses fit.


It is true that
the trees of the field
applied
          applause
                    apt
restrained.

Swimming
on land, flapping
wings non-existent
In the semblance of flight.

This would be what it would be to sing
this attest
        to
what my jaw was locked to.

To what my eyes failed to see.


The day was bright
and my mouth was burning
to walk on egg-
        shells something has to
        break. Strong, delicate,
unmoving, unmoored,
unsung, heard
in a barrel
        rolled.


Fold, felled, field
they have rainbows
there
        sometimes
a concentration of dust,
fumes, smoke:
        no stars
        no messages,
substitute
        passages,
a puzzle with violence gilded,
to pass through in the making of the day.

In the making of the ways,

a new registration:

are these yours:

These are the things the poem
cannot have and cannot
do.


It's cold in June.
And sometimes the
fulcrum
is a
phantom
        dangling
squeaking
        shouting
with no mouth.

It is true
        that
                I
collapsed
the out of order table
saluting with screen
the temple scream
of law.


Did the poem improve,
or was it weighed down
by too much stony air.
Seeing many things, and turning on its own premise,
did it promise continuance or demise,

did it ask the right questions of itself?


      The poem in prose,
       leadership material,
or did it hang back and follow
as a camp follower,
picking up scraps, mourning losses
that could not be named,
scrabbling in the dirt
for scraps of song that could be bought back,
a write-off, a debt
exchanged.


It was coloured glass,
and the colour of that glass in the room in the corner
was coloured green.


Filtered
      the water,
rendered quiet
      the splash,
      the thump,
      the flood.

This, too big,
after a period of waiting:

I was a passenger
or a visitor
or a leader
a guide

with the map up-
side wrong.

I cradled it to burst,
I warmed it at the flame,
I counted error first,
seeing
    if

           fingers
           would
    fit

singed;
With blinkers half-
slipped down the face,
these things I saw

Titles, squares, orbs, blocks,
boards
Fences, broken
houses,
    horses
           un-
seated
running
washed in flame.

Finally,
as at first,
What I said
burned out.
In the orbit
of the ambit

Tiles, squares, error.

My back collapsed
My voice went on.

# MORPHING LIFE

## PROXIMATE WOUNDING

Have you proclaimed
Proximate wounding.

Golden Schubert gobbet stuck on the brain.

I could do this, or that, poem says neither, either, we take both
forks to fade regret, maintain chance,
    (we can do that here)—

This song to be a room leading to another room no end, not
a song or a room the shell adding soft noise to the ear.

      Bruce
Springsteen
      on a horse,
a host of wild herds, a stadium or a cubby hole bolthole
cupboard to the side, repeating the same line over and over,
lullaby for us, still small and terrible, gentle.

      Spruce,
splice,
      spool.

Singing absence in obligation, let us now praise the tenuous
thread links dead to living breath. Fly to the sea, fade fast
morning's return. Alba, aubade, in the pocket a soul's fiction
I have as a gift, in the long sigh the trees breathe as they fall.

Misplacing my feet, again; again, glebe, globe, the profits
reserved. Where are we? Where we are, playback don't divulge,
reversing sounds, birds, cranes, voices; you should listen, you
should do so. Organised chance collective /

Stepped aside. As shores to groves to the bewitching pool where we leave them all alive.

If you pass by,
Call my name

# POEM (YOU CAN BE VIGILANT IN THE MORNING)

You can be vigilant in the morning,
keeping wake, keeping watch
without speeches

You can be vigilant in the afternoon
even, if you wake later in the flood,
hoping that the apparition of the lost meadow flowers
will return in the evening, if you evenly space your waking
to work or war

You can be vigilant at night
dark hour, half-light
temporarily unburdened

You can be vigilant around the grave
and it is open,
Disappearing into tokens
distributed with care

and the sky opens
and the flowers
already wilting
sing

# OCTOBER

You wake up
     and it is the morning
You wake up
     and it is the afternoon
You wake up
Fall in
     Leave the house

Window cracked across the skyline
clouds turning grey
over trees turning red;
Autumn day the sun a ghost bene-
     volent-
ly glowing over red
red sky
for a moment
     warm
before the cold
     calm
before the storm

Hard Facts in red
red autumn
*Hard Facts* in autumn
in red
*communist sparrows*
escape to the heights / pulled down
as the eye breaks in flight

two thousand and seventeen
one hundred years after anything
how does time get recorded

and how does it get lived

saw it in the distance
but still struggled to put it together

the question of tactics
        in words
of tactics
        in a poem
and what this means outside it

What we can do within the hours within the
seasons the
fixed limit

go to the next page

# YEAR'S MIDNIGHT

Where could you go
with your voice snowed in
frozen word, brittle, seasonal,
what looks forward with
audaciousness out of place,
a spacious room we'd fill full of the
provisional makes provision,
bridges burning, burned, repaired
the chorus in layers crying cracked;

Held hands and hearts
on hold, connection tenuous,
tenacious, pleading
don't let this day break,
life line, warming to whatever's earned
in the morning sun

To walk without thought of debt
as sucked-out air
of careless declaration
forms a tentative bridge,
soft surround
I've touched, swallowed, been
breathed through by,
cut apart
in;

To see a world made up of incision, injury,
to say, simply,
that you had a steady life
in the dying light
life like

but nothing like life

If you wait for me
I will tell you
Taking shelter on the brink
A house of twigs of sticks of leaves
Of solid concrete ripped apart
The birds trilling on top
in the trees at night

In the possibility to go on
stammering disconnections
for what gives, already gave
gives out or stays
Whatever briefest haven,
whatever pressured point

empty city full city, fell out obliquely
I feasted
I fasted
With others went on

as a single cloud in the opening sky before the fall of dusk
offers a
compass un-encompassed, point of rotation
outside measurable atlas,

Whether you call it the lovely lonesome voice or
the lovely lonesome void,
Whether you call it the waiting expectation,
*onset resurrection*
Whether you call it or call at all

If I wait for you

I will tell you
If you wait for me
I will tell you who I am

# THEY DRAW YOU A PICTURE OF QUIET

Do not let me be alone at night,
do not doubt
that night will suck labour dry
As Sleep prepares the labouring way
even sleep is not safe

With such
Gross
Trembling of hands
Where body protests with speech un-said
—un-thought—trails ever off.

Not the calloused hands but the calloused heart:
It is not the same. It is not the same. It is—the same:
Without spectacles, wrecked,
The voices sing along in the next room:
As even the dead cannot be left in sleeping peace.
But no one can be left without their dreams.

No chance—no choice—
things were already painted to be this way,
ending peacefully
absurd lights, stars, beacons,
buoys, the lights of earth and faint hill fires;

Fuck it—you write for whom—
I write poems for my friends
For those held close
and it breaks all the time.

In the same fixed place, the light still shines.
It stares unremittingly into the cold, cold night.

*

They draw you a picture of quiet
but beneath crackles sound
Picture of a flaw above the letters
Picture of a day's decent rest

Smuggled
in temporary occupance
In temporary tenancy
the objects that buttress belief

There is the new door inside an old door
a glimpse in the range of shadows
invisible light of the ghosts
we hoped to leave.

In the building re-
occupied, brutality of luxury,
uttered trace.

Making quiet sounds in the cage,
we moved in the outflow,
a dark glass premonition of what comes
detained, unimaginably left to dry or rot or freeze,
to lull in balm though temporary
and so to tell of ease.

*

To say that hope is a landing
or a moving; to stay and say
this here, *this* side;
or fugitive in the folding-in that protects,
out in the streets, letting it all fall out in the sun
that offers not much more than a place;

To step off of where we are
absolute: without absolution
another reminiscence
that multiplies fragments and silences
other spaces, other heavens
the possibility of not saying farewell

What is demanded of your presence
what is invoked, together and parting
can be unspoken, and be no demand
but spoken / on lines
holding / against harm,
hoping / against hope

in shattered fragments

in solid decay

\*

And me I know the least
excavating
for cause

what extends beyond con-
venience, beyond
figure of speech

So bending to believe
to dream
to be held by what light
swings out
against the dark.

Grasping at what, hardest to say,
is most deeply shared
on tongues that peak unspoken
on tongues that speak and slide
between our teeth

*

Absence of light. the stones
uprooted. the paving stones,
earth rolled and mashed
crashed and burned
and closed up again,
the clamour, clanging shout, smashed,
locked shut, but still the thing
glowing. still, in absent dark,
undergirding what would
shake the foundations,
break, spring up again, as

My eyes will never run dry,
never again return to that place,
and always return, always hover
on the splendour
of the chink of light still showing,
gravely, bright and slender:

The splendour of that brink

> *So softly tell your woe,*
> *adjacent to the main building closed.*

> *Till the bulb breaks,*
> *the light remains*
> *Stays flickering shape*

# MORPHING LIFE

*Is every night further claim laid upon our bodies to undo our*
        *brains,*
is day, anxious dread dread morning steals, and things change,
sun beats ordinance into body, into brain.
Against nature to make play, exchange roles,
spread out against sky's vast bed for sight,
fixed stars unfixed, sorrowful distance,
the falling drop, whatever gets you by,
tries so hard to deny or buffer against the
day so soon will fall, in
which so soon we'll fail

*

Sadness, motives, resentment, debt.
The sky is overhead.
Walk down the street.
Sing it over and over, lullaby for us,
still small and terrible, gentle.

Where are we? It's not safe.
Voice of acceptance.
Turn once more.
As shores to groves to the
bewitching pool where we
leave them young. That other life.

*

I thought of joy and antagonism,
a dream as clear as representation.

I thought of distance and the
lonesome miles the rain calls into question.

I thought that sometimes we made it
And sometimes we felt it falling from us
That sometimes we nailed it, naysaying in affirmation;
Got stuck, emerged, fleeting, fleeing, in sudden fluttered flourish
furiously believing.

By practice, and study, and the searing holding
of truth in patience, I thought that sometimes we hit
a precious and fragile pitch
beyond excitement
beyond endorsement

I thought it was hope.

Living to write to live
wishing that totality be not misery,
admitting the fractures,
Repeating in elegy
the vain, sustaining image,
imperishable love,
against such perishable absence
perpetually raises hand
to mouth;

      The terror by night,
      The ends, the means.

I thought I knew.

I thought I knew better.

I thought we could make it.

I thought it was hope.

I thought we could speak.

I thought we could try.

# NONE OF THEM IS GOING TO BE ALLOWED
# EVEN TO THINK OF THESE THINGS

Maybe we find it—maybe like love like poetry
like love conflicted—
in contradiction dumbfounded
without conditions or the
conditions for its existence unwrought—
wrenched out—strenuously sought
      and laid out—
as power balances out—
            curves away—
against hope hoping that each gesture reproves,
removes the poses that gender is—
          proposes—
ever believing not knowing all that knowing false sentiment—
held absolutely—cast out—
             unpaid—
the planet backs this—with division intact—
you learn the poses—
remoulded just to live in bare minimum subscribed—
as unacknowledged parts make piece
make work make parts of us—
                made law—
all in lives to live and daily be broken—
eaten—subsumed—subsisted—
            but not all—
that with fierce clinging in the wind—
with fierce hunger sated never be the song—
a commune—
        gone wrong—
the falling—
    the failing—
elsewhere in what unit moulded modelled care—

that no one be excluded—
despite assault from without—
                    assault from within—
in relation dumbfounded—
that against conditions of absolute harm
be bulwark be blinded reminded to try
rescinded provision strike out against it—
in life learn hard in error to teach it—
                              unacknowledged—
it can be discounted or held to—
held broken in part in
minute terror, particular touch—
that touch so tender, rubs rough—
hangs on.

# NOTES

'A True Account'.
Written after Cops off Campus demonstration, London, December 2013. *La classe operaia va in paradiso / The Working Class Goes to Heaven* (1971, dir. Elio Petri). Previously unpublished.

'Whatever You Think The Good Home'.
Epigraph from A.B. Spellman, 'for my unborn & wretched children', *The Beautiful Days* (The Poets Press, 1965). With the exception of the first poem, this sequence was first published as a chapbook by Punch Press in 2014.

'Against Nature'.
"One should live as long as is humanly possible"; "The work departs from you". Viktor Shklovsky, translated by Shushan Avgayan, *A Hunt for Optimism* (1931; translation published by Dalkey Archive, 2012). "all order, and beauty, luxury, peace and pleasure. Luxury and / voluptuousness." Charles Baudelaire, *'L'Invitation au Voyage'*, *Les Fleurs du Mal* (1857/1868). "This strategy sounds suspiciously like the programme of the counterrevolutionary party of the parliamentary bourgeoisie in the Second Empire." Geraldine Friedman, *The Insistence of History: Revolution in Burke, Wordworth, Keats, and Baudelaire* (Stanford University Press, 1996). This poem, along with 'Love is a Dangerous Necessity', was salvaged in 2022 from a series of poems written in 2014 on landscape-format A4 pages called at various points either *Landscape Poems* or *Everybody's Birthday All at Once*.

'The Problem, The Questions, The Poem'.
Epigraph from Leonard Wheatcroft, *A History of the Life and Pilgrimage of Leonard Wheatcroft of Ashover* (1627-1706), in *A Seventeenth-Century Scarsdale Miscellany*, Vol. 20 (Derbyshire Record Society, 1993). All other quotations submerged. *The*

*Problem, The Questions, The Poem* was originally published by Tipped Press in 2015.

### 'Aesthetics of Resistance'.
Pieter Bruegel the Elder first painted a version of the *Massacre of the Innocents* shortly after a catastrophically cold winter during the Eighty Years' War. "Shortly after its creation, the painting came into the possession of the Holy Roman Emperor, Rudolph II, in Prague. The slaughtered babies were painted over with details such as bundles, food and animals so that, instead of a massacre, it appeared to be a more general scene of plunder." This poem was first published alongside work by Lisa Jeschke, Lucy Beynon, and Tom Allen in the privately distributed *Violent Girlfriend* (2016).

### 'For Lectures'.
Quotations from Stephen Rodefer, *Four Lectures* (The Figures, 1982), and from a concert announcement by Charles Mingus. This sequence was first published in a privately distributed small run in 2016.

### 'From Sappho And Rilke'.
The final stanza of the third part of 'Morning Song' riffs off Rilke. "Punished in coitus" in the 'First Elegy' paraphrases a fragment from Kafka's journals set by György Kurtág in his *Kafka-Fragments*. The first part of 'Sappho' consists of fragments relating to Sappho and the suicide from the lover's rock: Euripides, Anacreon, Menander and Sappho herself. "Once I threw...the time" [Menander]; "Once more I dive...with love" [Anacreon]; "Not sacred...mortal dread" [Euripides, Cyclops]; "It is luxury I love...charade" [Sappho]. "*Not Sappho*" is from Muriel Rukeyser's 'Poem out of Childhood'. I have also worked off Julia Dubnoff's Sappho translations. These poems were mainly written in September 2015, and first appeared in *To the Reader* (Shit Valley, 2016).

**'Love is a Dangerous Necessity'.**
The title to this poem is taken from a piece by Charles Mingus recorded in 1970 and first released on the album *Pithycanthropus Erectus*. This poem, along with 'Against Nature', was salvaged in 2022 from a series of poems written in 2014 on landscape-format A4 pages called at various points either *Landscape Poems* or *Everybody's Birthday All at Once*.

**'October'.**
In October 2017, 100th anniversary of the October Revolution, Storm Ophelia blew aeolian mineral dust from the Sahara Dust across the ocean, causing a red daytime sky over London. *Hard Facts* is the title to Amiri Baraka's 1975 book of poetry (Peoples War / the Revolutionary Communist League (M-L-M), 1975). "*communist sparrows*" is quoted from the poem 'Red Autumn' in the same volume.

**'Year's Midnight'.**
"*onset resurrection*". Ed Marshall, 'Leave the Word Alone' (1955), first printed in *Black Mountain Review* in 1957.

**'Morphing Life'.**
"*Is every night further claim laid upon our bodies to undo our brains*". Jack Sharpless, 'Graveyard Shift', written during the 1980s and first published posthumously in *Chicago Review*, 1999, and collected in *Working Stiffs* (The Song Cave, 2014).

**'None of Them is Going to be Allowed even to Think of these Things'.**
This poem, along with elements of 'Morphing Life', was salvaged in 2021 from a largely unpublished sequence called *Dedications* originally written in 2014.